Attacking Soccer

a tactical analysis

by
Massimo Lucchesi

Published by
Reedswain Inc.

**Library of Congress
Cataloging - in - Publication Data**

by Massimo Lucchesi
   Attacking Soccer : A Tactical Analysis

ISBN No. 1-890946-71-0
Lib. of Congress Catalog No. 2001096710
© 2001

Editing
Bryan R. Beaver

Printed by
DATA REPRODUCTIONS
Auburn, Michigan

Reedswain Publishing
612 Pughtown Road
Spring City, PA 19475
800.331.5191
www.reedswain.com
info@reedswain.com

CONTENTS

PREFACE

If I were asked to pick out a match from all those that I have watched, I would have to choose Italy's 3–2 victory against Brazil at Sarrià in 1982. More recently I would select the splendid match at Old Trafford between Manchester United and Real Madrid (2–3) in 2000. As a neutral spectator I will always remember the nerve wracking semi-final between Germany and France during the 1982 World Cup, which ended 5-4 after the comeback by the Germans, or again the 3-2 victory of the French over Brazil in Mexico 1986. These were all matches of an extraordinary emotional intensity, contested by top class players who loyally confronted each other in an attempt to score that one extra goal that would guarantee the final victory for their team. They were all matches full of goals.

Goals are the magic of soccer. A goal is that strange thing that can make the thousands of people present in a stadium jump to their feet as one, and with them all those others that are watching the match in bars or at home in an armchair in front of the TV. A goal is that flash that unites millions of people all over the country, who will roar out their joy or their despair as the occasion demands. A goal is an extraordinary charge of emotion, which can generate an otherwise almost unthinkable explosion of collective energy – positive or negative as it may be. A goal breaks down all kinds of barriers, evoking the same reactions from people of different creeds, social classes, culture and origin. A goal is a work of art with the superb finishing touches from the free kicks of Del Piero and Zidane. A goal notched up by Inzaghi or Raul is a feat of cunning. A goal is an act of power as in the free kicks of Mihajlovic or Batistuta. A goal is pure class as in the one scored by the incomparable Maradona against the English during the World Cup in 1986 or Van Basten's incredible lob shot that went over the head of the Russian Dasaev and gave the Dutch national team the title of European champions in 1988. For all of us that have played soccer on the fields in the suburbs or at school, a goal has always been the means to make us feel as if we, too, were just a little Pelè, a Cruijff, a Platini, a Maradona, a Van Basten, a Baggio, a Figo, a Vieri or a Shevchenko. A goal can be a lot of things, but in the end it all comes down to this: goals are the magic of soccer.

The book that you are about to read aims to be an instrument in the hands of coaches, experts or even supporters, which, by way of a tactical analysis of the attacking phase of play, will help to understand and develop match strategies directed at goal scoring and victory, which are the surest ways of generating deep emotion in the 'soccer tribe'.

MASSIMO LUCCHESI
m.lucchesi@allenatore.net

1

THE PRINCIPAL TACTICAL ELEMENTS OF THE ATTACKING PHASE

A DEFINITION OF THE ATTACKING PHASE AND ITS PRINCIPAL CHARACTERISTICS.

The attacking phase of play is defined as the tactical situation when one team is in possession of the ball with the clear intent of approaching the opponent's goal.

The principal characteristics of a good attacking phase are the following:

1. **UNPREDICTABILITY**: that is, the team's ability to use the whole range of attacking techniques (which will be explained below), modifying or varying them constantly in order to put the opponents under constant pressure.
2. **EFFECTIVENESS**: the attacking phase, apart from being varied and unpredictable, must above all be effective. The real effectiveness of the attacking phase can be shown by the percentage of goals scored by the team. Of course each player on the team contributes to its goal scoring average, but the overall figure will always depend on those whose principal job it is to attack and strike at goal. In other words, in order to maximize the effectiveness of the offensive phase, the attacking strategy adopted must be based on the particular characteristics of the principal strikers on the team. Only then can we determine the best schemes that will put them in the position of being able to score.

3. **ADAPTABILITY**: as we have seen, the team must be unpredictable and effective; but it is also important that it can construct an attacking phase that can meet the many variables, whether tactical or otherwise, which it will have to face. The offensive play of the team will therefore have to adapt itself to the ground characteristics of the playing field, to the weather conditions and above all to the type of play used by the opponents. Let me try to clarify these concepts with a few examples. If, for example, the ground is uneven it will be more difficult to keep possession of the ball and it will also be important that the defense should avoid running unnecessary risks; it being, therefore, more difficult to organize long build-up plays, the team should opt for quick attacks based on a reduced number of passes in a vertical rather than a horizontal direction. The same general rule applies if the field is a particularly small one, or if the weather conditions have left the ground difficult to play on or slippery. On the contrary, if the temperature is high, it will usually be better to attack by adopting more elaborate operations in order to allow the team to move forward in a homogeneous way, so avoiding the useless waste of energy that could be brought about by a match played at a speed and intensity which might be impossible to keep up in the long run, and which would, therefore, have negative effects on the final result. It is of course important also to adapt our own play to that of our opponents', assessing how they prefer to attack in order to put ourselves in the position of being able to steal the ball and set up a counter attack (note that, as we will see later, the construction of an attack will normally vary in relation to the part of the field and the section of the team that recovers the ball). Apart from anticipating where it will be possible to regain possession of the ball in order to coordinate counter attacking moves, it is also a good idea to look carefully at the strengths and weaknesses of our opponent's defense system, both from a collective point of view and from that of each individual player. The considerations arising from this analysis will allow us to adjust our attacking

schemes to our opponent's defensive system so that we can 'strike' where they are weakest. However, though it may be a good idea to adjust the characteristics of our attacking play to our opponents, we should never convert our own philosophy into something totally unrecognizable just to meet another team.

To sum up, we can say that a good attacking system should be:

1) *Unpredictable* – and unpredictability, we must remember, is something that can be learned and improved.
2) *Effective* – and its effectiveness will partly depend on the ability of the coach to organize attacking play that makes the most of his players' strengths.
3) *Adaptable*, to a certain extent, to the strengths and weaknesses of the opponents.

THE RELATIONSHIP BETWEEN THE ATTACKING PHASE AND THE DEFENSIVE PHASE, AND THE INFLUENCE THAT THIS RELATIONSHIP HAS ON WAYS OF DEVELOPING AN ATTACKING GAME.

The attacking phase is not a tactical situation that can be taken by itself, independent of the phase when the opponents have possession and our team is defending. The two phases are in fact closely connected, and the quality of the attacking phase will depend on that of the defense and vice versa. To be as clear as possible about this, here are a couple of examples: if our opponents are attacking and putting us under heavy pressure, then we will very likely have to recover the ball in the defense zone (near the penalty box), and, in order not to run unnecessary risks, play a long pass in an attempt to set up a counter attack; on the contrary, if we manage to block the other players and recover the ball in the midfield, then it will be easier to develop a quick and more organized counter attack.

Our team's ability to defend with efficiency has a great influence on the way in which we develop the attacking phase. Even the number of players who can be involved in the attacking phase will depend, not only on the technical ability of the individuals or on the competence of the team in general in maintaining posses-sion of the ball, but also on the part of the field where the ball is recovered. If our team organization, and our ability in defense, allows us to regain the ball at a good distance from the goal we are defending, then we will be better able to redirect play with a good measure of calm and without taking unnecessary risks. It goes without saying that the closer we are to our own goal when we recover the ball, the higher the pressure we will be under and the lower our chances of playing it with the necessary compo-sure, because, if we lose the ball in such a situation we will be putting ourselves in clear and obvious danger.

Lastly, it is important to remember that the more players we can involve in the offense phase the more extensive our attacking front will be, thus offering us more solutions of assault, and put-ting the opposition's defense under greater pressure.

THE IDEAL PLACEMENT OF PLAYERS IN THE ATTACKING PHASE.

The placement of the players who are involved in the attacking phase must be such that it allows the entire team to exploit the whole attacking front (in both width and depth) in such a way as never to give precise points of reference to the opponents.

The main characteristics of attacking play must therefore be the following:

1. **Taking advantage of width**: the team must be able to move the ball exploiting the entire width of the playing field. Obviously, the more space the defending team is trying to cover the more difficult it is for them to do so efficiently. Encompassing play and lateral attacks are fundamental when you are facing a team that is digging itself into its own half of the field.

2. **Taking advantage of depth**: the ability to attack the opponent's defense by the strikers' movements in depth is one of the most important ways of putting pressure on a defense, which is lined up at a distance from its penalty box. Clearly the angle

of penetration (cuts) created by the attacking players will vary in relation to the depth of the defending team. If there is a good deal of space between the defensive line and the goal then vertical runs are possible; otherwise angled or even diagonal cuts are more effective.

3. **Unpredictability**: this is created by the team's ability to diversify the type of attacking plays that it uses.

We can achieve attacking moves in width or depth by:

- Placing the players in lines.
- Mobility of the players themselves.
- Distancing the players in the best possible way.

In an attacking phase it is important that possible ball receivers be lined up on various rhombi (or double triangles) of play.
The '**rhombus of play**' (which we will be looking at in more detail later) is an important means of moving the play forward, allowing the player with the ball who is looking towards the goal to pass it to the right or left at various depths. At the same time the player who receives with his back to the goal can release to the right or left, giving a lead pass in relation to the initial point of attack.
It is vital as well that the players should be mobile, not stationary. Mobility complicates life for the defender who is marking. It becomes difficult for him to position himself and takes away his points of reference, making the attacking moves unpredictable and therefore more effective.
Keeping the right distance between the players is another important way of getting the most out of attacking play. For example, we might decide to create a penetrating attack by moving up a striker and inserting a midfielder into the space created by his forward run. In this case, we must remember that, in order to successfully bring off such a move, the midfielder must come forward at the right moment, having been from the start in an ideal position in relation to the forward who is making space for such a move.

TYPES OF PLAYS THAT CAN BE CARRIED OUT IN THE ATTACKING PHASE IN RELATION TO THE NUMBER OF PLAYERS THAT PARTICIPATE IN THEM.

The attacking phase can be characterized by various types of plays. These can be divided into three sections:

1. **Elaborate attack**. A maneuver that is carried forward principally on horizontal lines will require that the team moves as one unit and advances with the ball. The elaborate attack entails a relatively high number of passes, and calls for players capable of building up plays and surmounting the opponent's defensive lines through:
   a) creative, coordinated movements;
   b) the exploitation of the spaces between players, or,
   c) movements down the sidelines that will lead to a cross and so jump the defense.

2. **Maneuvered counterattack**. A play that develops principally in vertical lines through which the team tries to exploit, as quickly as possible, a space that has opened up. If a play like this is to be effective the players must be good at receiving the ball in deep positions, at creating passes that penetrate the free spaces and at moving forward with the ball at their feet, beating opponents, or changing speed or direction.

3. **Instant attack**. A type of play marked by the speed of its development. When the team gets possession of the ball it tries immediately to counter by turning the tables on the opponents. Of course, this type of attacking move gives the team more chance of finding its opponent's back defenders' line unprepared; but we must always remember that it also makes it very difficult to support the play, which means that, should the play fail, the team will find itself under pressure once again, not having been able to move up behind the ball.

For good players we would generally suggest alternating the elaborate attack with the maneuvered counterattack, falling back on the instant attack when, on regaining the ball, we notice that our opponent's defense lines are badly positioned or exposed. When playing on fields that are not always completely flat and with players whose technical abilities are not always up to the mark, we believe that the best tactic to use is the maneuvered counterattack.

A TACTICAL ANALYSIS OF THE ATTACKING PHASE.

Now that we have illustrated the characteristics of and the relationships between the various types of attacking phases, we can begin to analyze them from a tactical point of view. It is possible to subdivide the attacking phase into a number of sub-phases (each with its own characteristics and aims) in order to simplify the achievement of our principle objective – scoring goals.
The sub-phases which make up an attacking action are:

- Plays after gaining possession of the ball.
- Build-up of play.
- Final touches.
- Shooting.

DEVELOPING ATTACK AFTER GAINING POSSESSION OF THE BALL.

The first thing that the team which has regained possession of the ball must try to do is to consolidate this new situation and allow the players to spread themselves out so they will occupy the best spaces from which they can develop the attacking phase. The two things most necessary here are:

> **1.** tactical organization, and
> **2.** the individual's ability to maintain possession.

The player who has intercepted the ball can consolidate possession either by keeping it himself or by passing to a teammate who is in a better position to play it well.

We should never underestimate this sub-phase, following on regaining possession of the ball. In modern soccer more and more goals are scored as a result of quick, incisive actions subsequent to regaining possession of the ball in the opponent's midfield. As a result, moving instantly into attack as soon as the ball has been taken back into possession is clearly a detail that can make the difference. For the same reason, it is of the utmost tactical importance to organize the team in such a way that the player who has regained the ball, and who cannot counterattack immediately, finds, nevertheless, a certain amount of support nearby in order to pass it on to a teammate and so limit the effects of his opponents' pressing. In thinking about ways that will allow the team to exploit this sub phase fully it is, however, a good idea to look first at how the team has come back into possession of the ball.

Situations that give us back possession of the ball as a result of play having been stopped by the referee (fouls, offsides, balls that have been sidelined etc.) do not belong to the particular sub-phase that concerns us here. What we are talking about are exclusively plays following on the ball being 'stolen' from the opponents while still in play.

One more thing, when the player who has regained possession – whether by anticipating his opponent or by capturing a loose ball – has his face to the goal, he will be able (especially if he is in his opponent's midfield) to spark off a lightning counterattack. On the other hand, if he has his back to the goal or if he is to one side and cannot, for that reason, set up a quick attacking movement, it is important that the coach should have prearranged various solutions that will enable the players to move the ball forward with relative ease, so allowing the team to build up play.

BUILDING UP PLAY.

This is that sub phase of attacking play when the team which has possession is trying to approach its opponent's goalmouth. In general, it is possible to build up play in three different ways:

- Elaborate, or maneuvered build-up.
- Immediate build-up.
- Mixed build-up.

The **elaborate build-up** (typical of Brazilian teams, or teams whose players are at a good technical level) evolves for the most part through a series of short passes that allow the whole team to move forward with the ball.

The **immediate build-up**, on the other hand, involves moving the ball forward through a systematic use of long passes. We must point out that teams which employ this type of build up may get overbalanced if the midfielders can't control high balls or do not press their opponents effectively when they in turn counterattack. Though the immediate build up has a number of advantages (the most important of which is that the opponents will find it more difficult to steal the ball in our half of the field), its most evident drawback is that it will limit the number of solutions open to the striker or the strikers, because they will not always be able to rely on their teammates' support.

The **mixed build-up** requires the team to use both the long and the short pass in the attacking movement. This type of build up is convincing when the long pass precedes the short passes, while a maneuver that starts off with a number of short passes and finishes up with a long pass is to be considered tactically counterproductive.

In my opinion, the most intelligent and the most tactically interesting movements are the ones that begin with the long ball (keeping in mind that we must have players in the team capable of receiving this particular kind of pass and they can easily be anticipated by a defender), because, as we have already seen, it cuts down the risks of our team losing the ball in a dangerous part of the field. It is essential, however, that the team should be capable of following up this initial play with a more reasoned maneuver consisting of short passes so as to give all the players time to advance in support of the strikers, thus offering a wider range of tactical solutions when the moment comes to lay on the final touches.

But now, having seen and analyzed the various types of build up, we can have a closer look at the tactical organization we can give the team in this delicate sub phase.

Elaborate build-up.
In order to build up a reasoned maneuver the player in possession of the ball must have a number of tactical choices open to him, always keeping in mind the position of his body in relation his primary objective (to make the ball move forward).

If the player in possession has his face towards the opponents' goal his teammates must make it possible for him to carry out:
a) an oblique pass to another player in front of him;
b) a more or less vertical pass to a player in an even more advanced position;
c) a diagonal pass in the opposite direction to the one from which he received the ball, with the aim of widening the attacking front; or even
d) a back pass to a player behind (F_1).

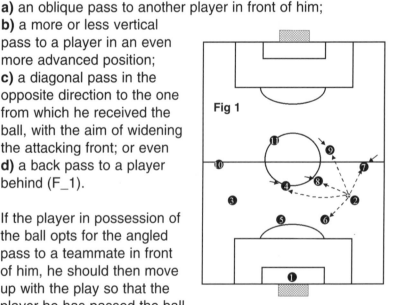

Fig 1

If the player in possession of the ball opts for the angled pass to a teammate in front of him, he should then move up with the play so that the player he has passed the ball to can pass it back to him if necessary (F_2). By moving up he will have liberated a part of the field into which his teammate can pass the ball back to him, but he will also have added dynamism to the play and taken away valuable points of reference to the defenders.

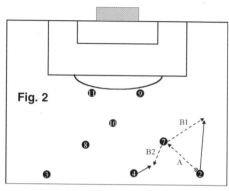

Fig. 2

However, the player in possession will not always be able to pass to a teammate in front of him, and he will not always be able to move up so that he can receive the ball back. When we are playing in our own midfield, or even worse, in the area around our own penalty box, and the ball is at the feet of a defender, it might be risky if he were to advance because this would free a space for a possible counterattack if a teammate loses the ball. In cases like these, the player (especially if he is a defender) should pass to a teammate who is nearer to him, or cross the ball diagonally, opening up new perspectives for the movement. When the player decides to pass the ball in a vertical direction, the receiver, who will presumably have his back to the goal, must be able to dump it to a player just below him (F_3).

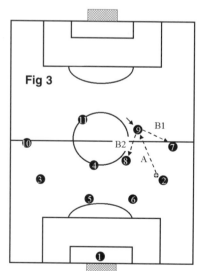

Fig 3

If the tactical organization permits this player to dump the ball, and if his timing is right, then the action will have advanced in reference to the point from which it began, and the player now in possession (facing the goal) will find himself in the same tactical situation and with the same choices open to him as those which we have already discussed above. We have just mentioned two factors: tactical organization and timing. These are important because the player who receives a vertical ball will very probably have to move towards it in order to avoid the ball being intercepted by a defender. It is essential, therefore, that he has one or more immediate solutions open to him, otherwise, when he has controlled the ball, this player, with his back to the goal, will have to move too far down field before he can dump it on to a teammate.

Having looked at the ball receiver with his face or his back to the goal, we can now move on to look at one who takes possession after an angled pass, who will probably have his face and back to the sidelines.

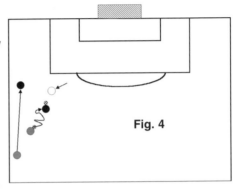

Fig. 4

If this player is unmarked, he will turn towards the goal and, apart from being able to count on the creation of a 2 on 1 situation by the up-field movement of the teammate who has just passed to him (F_4), he will be in the advantageous position of having his face towards the goal he is heading for.

If, however, he cannot turn in this way, other solutions must be open to him.

a) he might be to return the ball to his teammate who has moved up field in support (B).

b) he could make a diagonal back pass towards a player from his own section of the team who has come up in support (C);

c) the least advantageous solution (D) is that the possessor dumps the ball on another player who has come to take up the position of the player who has moved up-field (F_5).

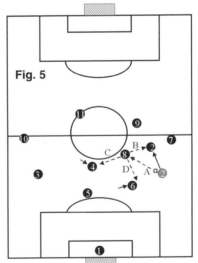

Fig. 5

If he decides for the second of these three possible plays, the player that he passes to will have his face towards the goal, and, apart from being in a position to apply the various options that we have just outlined, will also now be able to exploit the player that has moved up-field.

Having summed up all the various opportunities open to players according to the direction in which they are facing, we must now insist that the geometrical figure that allows play to develop along these lines is the rhombus (or the triangle, if the ball possessor is placed along the sidelines of the field).
We hope to demonstrate in the following examples that it is pre-cisely the ability of the team to draw up these triangles or rhombi on the field of play – which will allow for the development of good attacking play (F_6; F_7; F_8).

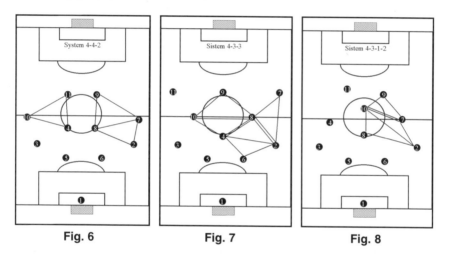

Fig. 6   Fig. 7   Fig. 8

The elaborate build-up can be developed along the lines that we have just seen in action, but it can also be successful even if its progress is much less organized. The Brazilians do not apply a highly programmed build-up, but, being technically skilled play-ers, they are, nevertheless, one of the best teams in the world because they are incredibly accurate in passing and in receiving the ball. Even if play is based more on technical than on tactical skills, however, it will have to be carried out on the basis of dynamic movement of the players on the entire attacking front and alteration between long/short and vertical/diagonal passes.

IMMEDIATE BUILD-UP.

The immediate build up can give good results only if you have players with certain particular strengths. First of all, the players at the back must be able to kick long balls. At the same time, the receiving players must be well up to the mark. We have already seen that it is by no means easy to receive a long ball, for two good reasons: firstly, the long ball gives the defender time to intercept; and secondly, it is difficult for the attacking player to control the ball in the air.

It is important, therefore, that the players whose job it is to receive should be either particularly good at controlling the ball in the air, or at receiving it along the ground. Note also that good measures taken by the defending team can make the attacking players' life even more difficult. If you want to limit the ability of a player whose job it is to gain ball possession in the air, it is very easy to put a defending player with the same skills in the position where the striker generally comes to jump; and taking control of the sidelines is a good tactical move if you want to create difficulties for an attacking player who prefers to receive along the ground.

FINAL TOUCHES.

Having now examined the various ways of building up play, and having illustrated the principle solutions in the figures, we can now pass on to another phase: the finishing touches.

The finishing touches are the phase in which the team tries to unmark a player so that he can shoot.

The building up phase has a great influence on the final touch phase, but now the opponents' defensive strategy will be of great importance too. A team that defends from a position at the limits of its penalty area will force its opponents to play encompassing movements ending up with a cross from the back line, or by combinatory movements between two players or by a long shot from outside the area. On the other hand, a team that prefers to defend in depth leaves space between the defenders and the goal, making it easier to cut during the final touches phase.

Those who think numerical superiority is the only important factor in shooting at goal are ignoring other situations in which it is possible to score:

It is possible to shoot at goal after:

- a ball stolen in attack.
- a long shot (with a high defense).
- an assist from a teammate.
- dribbling.

A goal can be sparked off by a ball captured in attack or as the result of a shot from far out with the opponents' defense lined up – and neither of the two necessarily require a situation of numerical superiority. We could say the same for a crossing pass that ends up as an assist.

Let us now focus our attention on two types of finishing touches: the assist and dribbling.

The assist – that is, a pass that will free a player from marking and allow him to shoot – can develop from one of the following attacking techniques.

- angled pass in depth (cut). (F_9)
- dump and rebound pass to allow the penetration of a player without the ball. (F_10)
- combination between two players. (F_11)
- in depth overlapping. (F_12)
- crossing. (F_13)
- pass to unmark a player as the defense moves back.

An in-depth pass to a player who is cutting in (the striker) assumes that the player without the ball has space to attack in front of him (and the more space he has the easier it will be to serve him) and that the player with the ball (the finisher) is good at passing the ball in such a way as to open up space. The nearer the finisher is to the striker the more precise the pass is likely to be.

When the opposing defense is closed around its penalty area it is very difficult for the finisher to cut the ball to the center, and in this case it is tactically more intelligent to pass externally and then to cross.

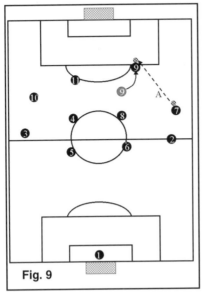

Fig. 9

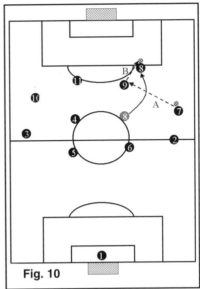

Fig. 10

One important point about cuts is this: even if a defending player manages to anticipate the ball he will still be facing his own goal and this will make it difficult for him to kick it away and free his area.

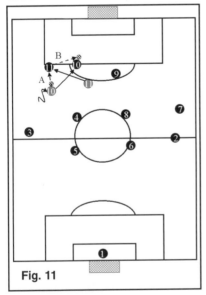

Fig. 11

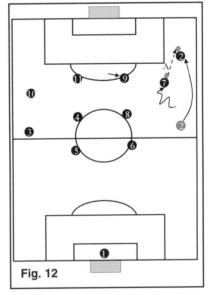

Fig. 12

One difference between a cut and a dump and rebound pass is that at the beginning of the play the receiver is nearer the goal

that he is attacking than the penetrating player, who will be the one to shoot.

The dump and rebound pass can be effective both when there is little space between the defense line and the goal and also when that space is greater. When space is limited the 'closed' dump and rebound pass is the best, with the penetrating player 'below' or very near the imaginary line on which the ball receiver is placed (see fig. 10). With more space behind the defense, 'open' wall passes are better, where the striker receives the ball above that line.

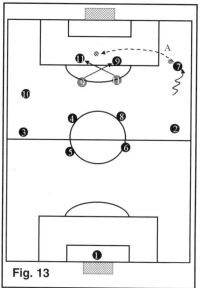

Fig. 13

The combination is similar to the dump and rebound pass. It involves two players and can be developed by a dump and rebound pass or a dummy movement. Classical combinations involving a double (or wall) pass are the 'give and go' or the 'give and follow'. As we have just seen looking at dump and rebound passes, the greater or lesser opening of the pass will depend on the position of the players and the playable space behind the defense.

Dummy movements are combinations between two players when the finisher gives an advantage to the striker by pretending to take possession of the ball, but really letting it arrive to his teammate. Dummy movements are good when play is tight.

At this point, having spoken of cuts, dump and rebound passes and combinations, we can conclude our study of finishing touch techniques by having a look at overlapping, crossing and assists.

Overlapping is a finishing touch technique halfway between the dump and rebound pass and the cut. As in the wall pass, in fact, the penetrating player who moves up to receive the pass starts off from a position behind the one who does the assist, while, similarly to the cut, the player who is about to pass the ball, opening up space and unmarking his teammate, is actually facing the goal.

Overlapping can be played both centrally or to the side. Central overlapping can usually be done in counterattack when the striker with the ball has managed to turn around and with a midfielder or a second striker who is penetrating from behind. On the contrary, overlapping along the sidelines is useful when you want to dis-unite the defenders and bring them wide, and it is a good way of bringing the team to a cross.

The cross is one of the finishing touch plays that does not require the team to be in numerical superiority before taking a shot on goal. With the cut, the dump and rebound pass, the combination and overlapping you generally try to create a 2 on 1 situation, or to free the striker from the control of his direct opponent (1 to 0). On the contrary, you can strike at goal from a cross even if you are being heavily marked. To transform a cross into a goal what the player needs, more than the ability to liberate himself of his marker, is a sense of timing and good elevation. As far as the rest of the team is concerned, the best way of increasing the effectiveness of crosses is to work on ways of occupying strategi-cally useful positions in the area without getting in each other's way.

Naturally, the ability of the strikers and their effectiveness in tak-ing command of space is not enough: the crosses themselves must be good!

The crosses that are most troublesome for the defense are those that go over their shoulders. When a finisher sees that there is the chance of putting the ball behind the defense he should cross at once, even if he can move further forward.

Crosses from the bottom of the field of play can be dangerous as well. In such cases, in fact, the attacking player can keep in clear sight both the part of the field from where the ball is coming and the part of the goal where he can try to place the ball.

Crosses are by far the most common of all finishing touch plays, and they are indispensable when you are facing deep defense systems drawn up around their own penalty area.

The last way of finishing up an attacking play is the assist into the area while the defending team is moving back.

More than a finishing touch play this is really a way of putting a player in a position to shoot. If the attacking team has come into numerical superiority, (as a result of the plays that we have just been looking at or by dribbling), the defending team will be forced to move backwards, opening up space to allow the strikers to receive an assist.

While the other plays that we have spoken about are true finishing touches, in a case like this we are simply using numerical superiority in order to free a player and allow him to strike.

2

THE PRINCIPAL ATTACKING SOLUTIONS OF THE 4–4–2 SYSTEM.

A definition of strategy, tactics, system and play.

We have now had a theoretical look at the tactics of the attacking phase, and, before going into a detailed examination of the plays of each single system, it might be a good idea to underline and explain exactly what we mean by strategy, tactics, system and play.

Strategy is the way in which the team performs in order to achieve its aims. By strategy, then, we mean the general guidelines by which the team regulates its play.

Tactics are a fundamental part of strategy. The team achieves its objectives by making the right tactical choices from the many variables connected with the game of soccer. Tactics and strategy are closely related. We could say this: while strategy defines the road to follow in order to arrive at our target, tactics are the way in which we move along that road.

The **system** defines the placement of the eleven players on the field. The system is usually expressed in numbers (**4-3-3, 4-4-2, 3-5-2, 3-3-3-1** etc.) to show how many players are placed in defense, in the midfield or in attack.

The **plays**, on the other hand, are the keys – the single procedures – utilized by the team in order to carry out its operations in defense and in attack. Plays are what bring the team to score goals in attack or to gain possession in defense. The team's tactics influence its plays: and, in fact, it is the tactical analysis of the match that will suggest the best plays for the team to use in attack or defense.

SYSTEM 4-4-2.

The 4-4-2 is probably the most frequently used system in soccer today. Its success is due to the fact that it gives a balanced placement of the players on the field, favoring good coverage and doubling up in defense, while at the same time giving the attacking team the chance to control the ball and utilize the whole attacking front.

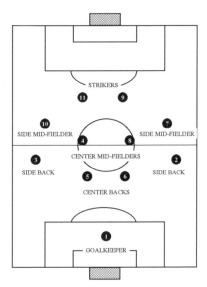

These are the main characteristics necessary in this system:

SIDE BACKS
• Excellent physique and speed.
• Good at tackling and at play in the air.
• Tactically flexible with a good ability to anticipate situations.
• Able to play both short and long passes.

CENTER BACKS
• Good stamina.
• Ability in supporting attacking play.
• Good skills in defense.
• Capable of organizing the defense in line.

SIDE MIDFIELDERS
- Good dribbling skills and/or good acceleration
- Able to create space for the penetration of the side back by moving towards the center of the field.
- Good at crossing from the bottom of the field and at passing the ball in depth.
- Consistent participation in the defense phase.

CENTER MIDFIELDERS
- Tactical intelligence.
- Ability in intercepting great numbers of balls
- Excellent tactical sense enabling him to organize the teams attacking play.
- Able to coordinate pressing.

STRIKERS
Apart from being able to work together, the individual strengths of each striker should complement those of the other.
A striker who is:
- skilled at protecting the ball
- good at heading the ball, and physically strong
- good in the area and able to create space

should have as his companion one who is:
- mobile and quick
- skilled in dribbling and with a good imagination.
- capable of shooting from a distance

THE PLAYS OF THE 4-4-2.

Intensity and organization: playing as a group in build up.

The team must be able to build up play with confidence, flow and variation. It is indispensable never to lose possession when the team is off balance (too far forward for example) or near or around the area. At the same time, play must be fluid and well-timed. Two touch plays will help the team to move the ball quickly and give consistency to the operations. The team must also diversify build up so that the opponents never have clear points of reference. In the following illustrations we will be looking at some examples of how to organize group movements in build up. We will be able to see how the player can move away from the ball, creating space for a teammate coming up to receive it at full speed.

A combination between the two center midfielders with the side mid fielder in possession.

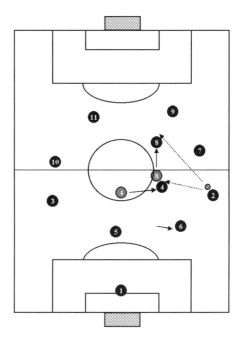

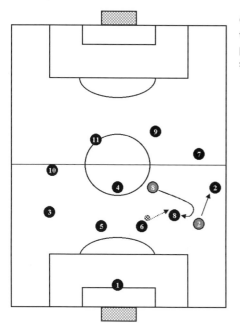

Combination between two center midfielders. Side back in possession, having two possible solutions open to him.

Combination between center midfielder and side back. Center back in possession.

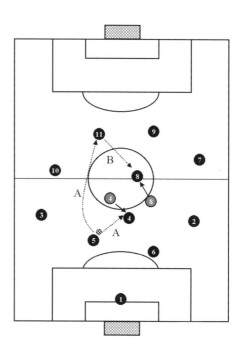

Combination between the two
center midfielders with center
back in possession.
The center defender can give
the ball to the number 4, or
make a long pass to the striker
with the number 8 moving up to
accompany play.

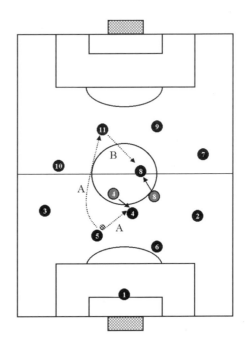

Combination between the two
side players. Center midfielder
in possession has two solutions
open to him.

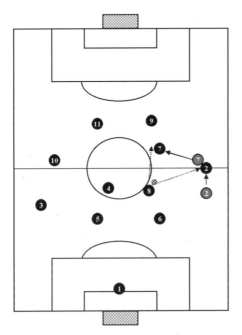

BUILDING UP PLAY WITH THE LONG PASS.

We have already looked at the advantages and disadvantages of this tactical play in building up attack. We show here some examples of how to build up play using the long pass.

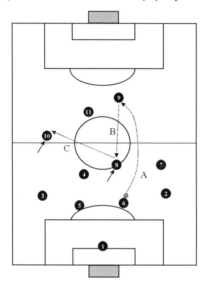

Immediate build-up: example I

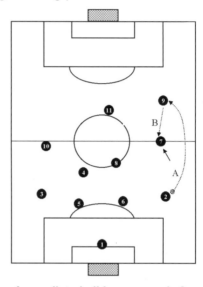

Immediate build-up: example 2

ELABORATE BUILD-UP.

Moving the ball around the area of defense.

It is vital that the team should 'move the ball behind' in order to set up attacking play. In this figure we see the ideal placement of the players in a semicircle or half moon and their interconnected passes. In the first pass the left side-back dumps the ball to the center side back who is behind and placed diagonally to the player in possession. The left side-back then passes to the right side-back, i.e., opening up the line of play. If he is not sure that he can do this he should opt instead for a long pass. Once he has possession, the right side-back can pass to a player to his right, who, having received the pass will be in a good position to move play forward.

Keeping the ball moving in the area.

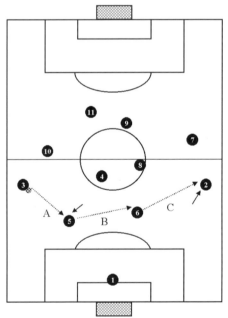

MOVING THE PLAY FORWARD FROM THE DEFENSE TO THE MIDFIELD USING DIAGONAL PASSES, OR VERTICAL PASSES FOLLOWED BY A DUMP.

Here we can see examples of how the team can move the ball forward from the defense to the midfield using diagonal passes, or vertical passes followed by a dump.

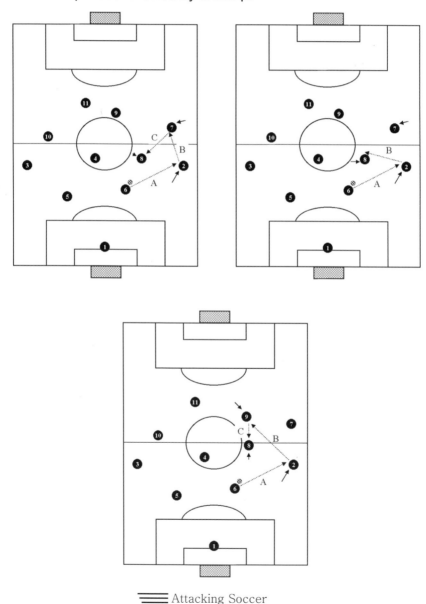

EXAMPLES OF HOW TO BUILD UP PLAY:

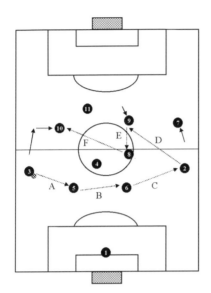

Elaborate build-up: example I

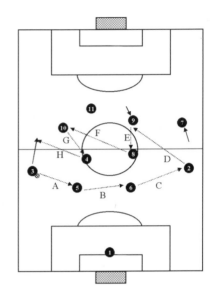

**Elaborate build-up: example I
I st Alternative**

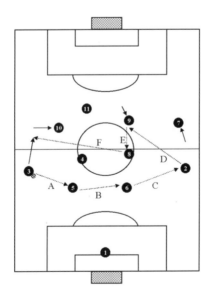

**Elaborate build-up: example I
2nd Alternative**

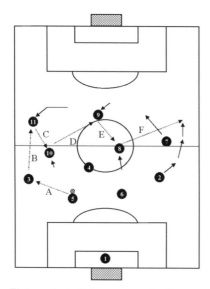

Elaborate build-up: example 2

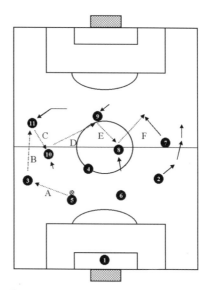

Elaborate build-up: example 2
1st Alternative

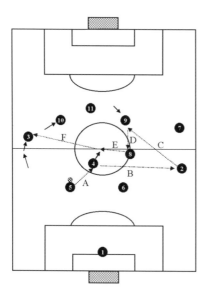

Elaborate build-up: example 3

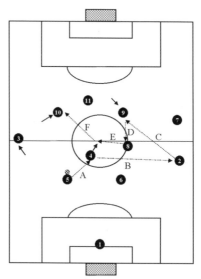

Elaborate build-up: example 3
1st Alternative

BRILLIANCE, ORGANIZATION AND COHESION IN THE FINISHING TOUCH PHASE.

We have already seen that the distinguishing features of attacking play are confidence, flow and variety. It is essential that the play should be quick, crisp and adapted to the opponents' weaker points. In the finishing touch phase it is vital that the players should move quickly and in time with each other. In the following figures we will be having a look at group movements during finishing touches. It is important to see how the joint movements of two or more advancing players can create space for another teammate to take possession and attack from there.

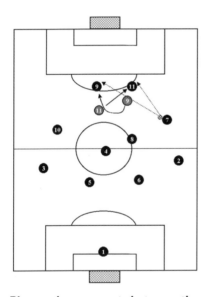 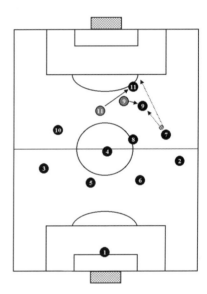

Plays and movements between the two strikers with the side midfielder in possession: he can pass to either of the forwards.

Plays and movements between the two strikers with the side midfielder in possession.

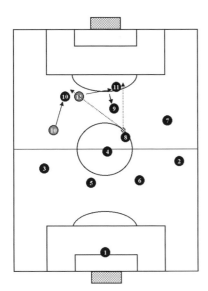

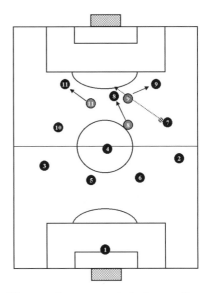

Plays and movements between a striker and the side midfielder. Center midfielder in possession: he can pass to either of the players.

Plays and movements between the strikers with the center midfielder moving up into the space created for him.

BREAKS.

This happens when a player steals the ball in his opponents' half.
This type of play can be very dangerous because the opponents'
defense will be unprepared and out of position. Having stolen the
ball the player in possession should keep it for a dribble or two so
that the strikers can sprint quickly forward.

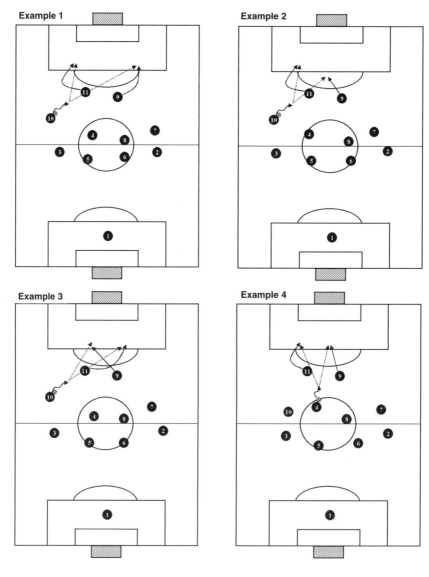

Example 5

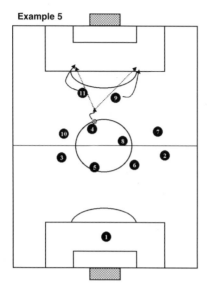

Example 6

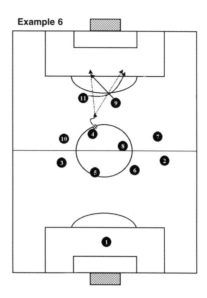

THE ATTACK IN DEPTH.

This is an attacking play that can be carried out when the opponents' defense line is not too deep. In a case like this, you can attack the space behind the defense with in-depth cuts. In the following figures we will be looking at cuts by players using the 4-4-2.

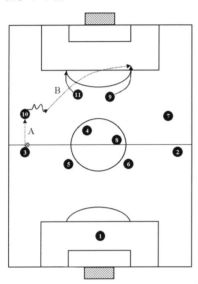

ATTACK IN DEPTH.
Cut: left side midfielder to right striker.

ATTACK IN DEPTH.
Cut: left side midfielder to left striker.

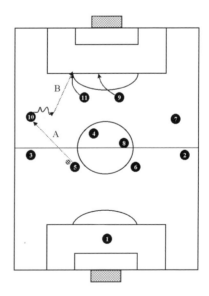

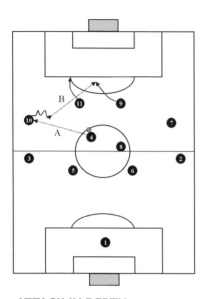

ATTACK IN DEPTH.
Cut: left side midfielder to right striker.

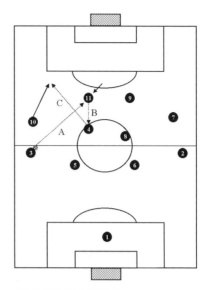

ATTACK IN DEPTH.
Cut: center midfielder to left side midfielder.

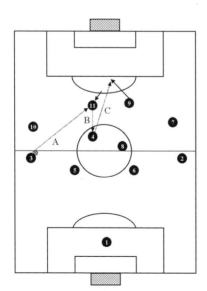

ATTACK IN DEPTH.
Cut: center midfielder to right striker.

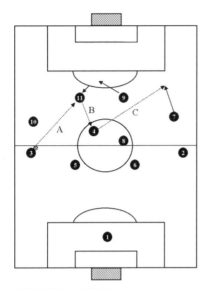

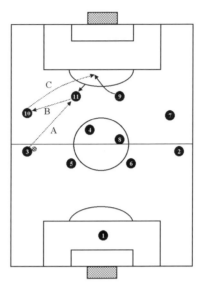

ATTACK IN DEPTH.
Cut: center midfielder to right side midfielder.

ATTACK IN DEPTH.
Left side midfielder to right striker.

SIDE ATTACK.

This type of play is necessary when a defense line is drawn up and you need to get around it on the outside. Enveloping play, combinations, dump and rebound passes and cuts are all useful ways of arriving at a part of the field from where you can cross efficiently into the area. In the following diagrams we will be looking at some examples of side attacks that can be developed using the 4-4-2.

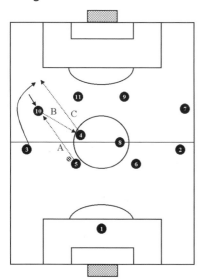

SIDE ATTACK.
Enveloping play: center midfielder to left back.

SIDE ATTACK.
Enveloping play: striker to left back.

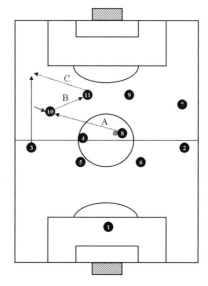

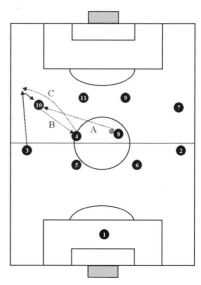

SIDE ATTACK.
Enveloping play: center midfielder
to left back.

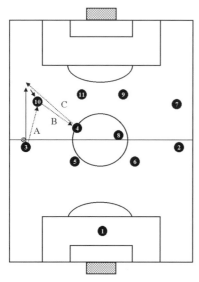

SIDE ATTACK.
Enveloping play: center midfielder
to left back.

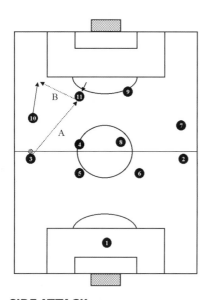

SIDE ATTACK.
Dump and rebound pass: striker to
left side midfielder.

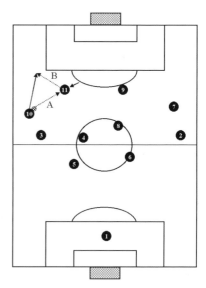

SIDE ATTACK.
Combination give and go: side player – striker – side player.

CENTRAL ATTACK.

A drawn up defense line can be attacked centrally using dump and rebound passes or combinations. Used as an alternative to side attacks, this type of play gives variation to the team. In the following diagrams we will see central attacks developing from dump and rebound passes or combinations.

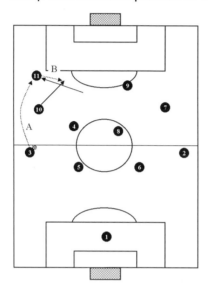

CENTRAL ATTACK.
Dump and rebound pass: striker to left side midfielder.

CENTRAL ATTACK.
Dump and rebound pass: striker to left side midfielder.

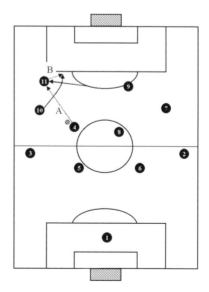

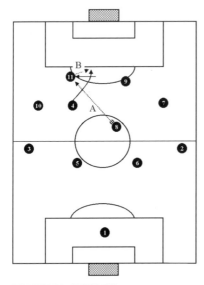

CENTRAL ATTACK.
Dump and rebound pass: striker to center midfielder.

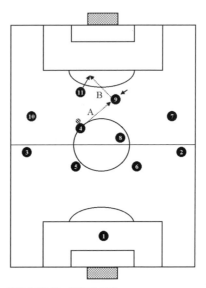

CENTRAL ATTACK.
Dump and rebound pass: right striker to left striker.

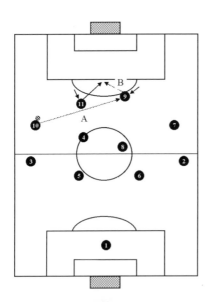

CENTRAL ATTACK.
Dump and rebound pass: right striker to left striker.

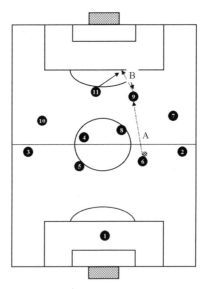

CENTRAL ATTACK.
Dump and rebound pass: right striker to left striker.

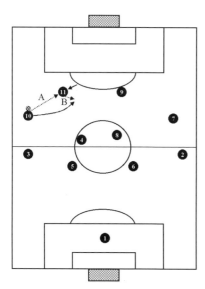

CENTRAL ATTACK.
Combination: give and follow, side player – striker –side player.

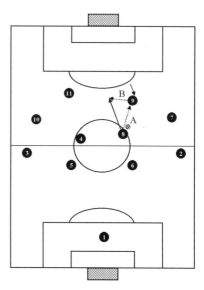

CENTRAL ATTACK.
Combination: give and go, center midfielder – striker – center midfielder .

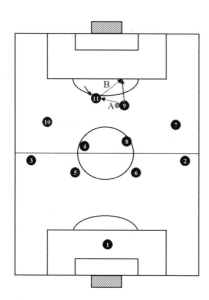

CENTRAL ATTACK.
Combination: give and go, striker – striker – striker.

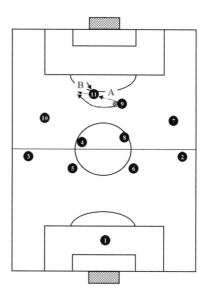

CENTRAL ATTACK.
Combination: give and follow, striker – striker – striker.

POSITION OF THE PLAYERS FOR A CROSS.

This is how the players should place themselves to receive a cross:

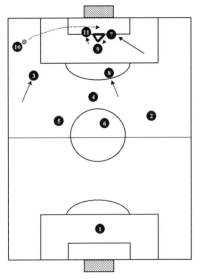

Example 1.
The left striker on the near post.
The side midfielder on the other.
The right striker in the central area.
The center midfielder covers the part of the field outside the area.
The side back is in support of the player in possession.

Example 2.
The left striker on the near post.
The right striker on the other.
The center midfielder in the central area.
The side midfielder covers the part of the field outside the area.
The side back is in support of the player in possession.

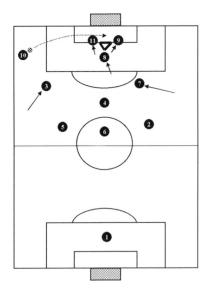

POSITION OF THE PLAYERS WHEN WINNING POSSESSION FROM A REBOUND.

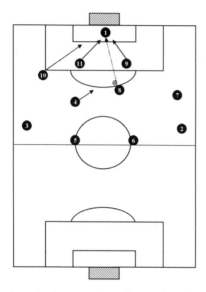

Example of placement after winning the ball.

FACING YOUR OPPONENTS' SYSTEM.

The 4-4-2 against the 3-4-1-2.

When you play against a 3-4-1-2 formation the most difficult problem to resolve is your opponents' attacking midfielder. This player moves between your defense line and the midfield, and can put you under terrible pressure. He is difficult to control as well, and to do so you will have to move the center midfielder back (that is, if the player in question has the necessary ability to limit this man's play). Naturally the team will then have problems in the midfield, where a single player will be facing the opponents' two.

Nevertheless, the two side backs will be free, and will be able to put greater pressure on their opponents, who, in their turn, will be facing two players. After gaining possession the team should try to develop play by passing along the sidelines so creating enveloping attacks that will force the opponents to move back, thus detaching the attacking midfielder from the vicinity of your area, where he is at his most dangerous.

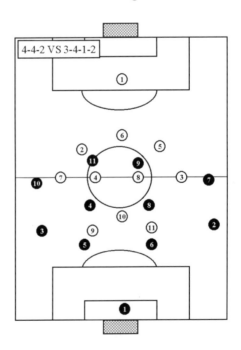

4-4-2 VS 3-4-1-2

The 4-4-2 against the 4-3-3.

The four backs are playing in numerical superiority against the three forwards. This creates an advantage in the defense phase, but it also makes it difficult for the backs to manage the ball.
In the midfield the four midfielders have to stop the opponents' three. Good and continuous pressing is important here, so as not to allow the opponents to pass in depth to the wings, who will then be able to create problems for the backs by penetrating with diagonal cuts between side and center players. It is a good thing, in fact, to make sure that the wings enter in possession only after short passes given directly to their feet. If they have to sprint forward to meet their passes, the side midfielder will be left behind and won't be able to double up with his teammate and help him mark the opponent. Also, when the team is building up play the ball should be passed to the side midfielders who must be positioned wide. This will make them difficult to mark, both for the opponents' center midfielder, (who will have to come too far to the sides), and for their side back, (who will have to come too far forward). In attack, two strikers play against four defenders, but they can use the two against two situations created in the center to put their opponents under pressure.

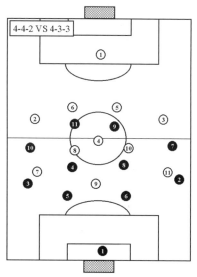

4-4-2 VS 4-3-3

The 4-4-2 against the 4-4-2.

This is a match in which the winning team will probably be the one with the better organization, technical quality and athletic preparation. Each team is the mirror image of the other, and the play will be full of individual contests.

Two pairs of players face each other on the sides and also in the midfield. One little tactical change that could be made is the choice of the player who is to support the two center backs when they meet the opponents' attack. Each team will have the same number of players involved in the plays. Wishing to avoid that, the side backs could keep wide of the ball, or you could move one of the center midfielders down.

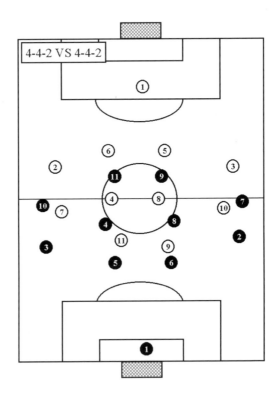

The 4-4-2 against the 3-5-2.

The four players of the defense are lined up against the opponents' two center strikers. Numerically, the midfield is inferior to the opponents. And in attack our two strikers have to win against three defenders. Here, the work of the side backs is vital, and they must make sure that our two center backs never end up in a two against two situation against the opponents' strikers.
It is important at the same time that the side backs should keep play going once they have possession, because, of course, they will have more freedom. The four side players (two side backs and two side midfielders) must enter continually into play because they will be marked by only one opponent player in their zone. In cases like these, good build up is very important in order to keep the opponents in their own half and force them to play under pressure.

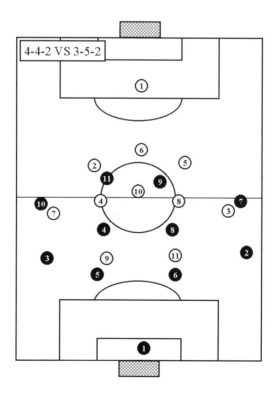

4-4-2 VS 3-5-2

The 4-4-2 against the 3-4-3.

The defense plays in numerical superiority against the strikers. In the midfield the number of players are the same while the two strikers play against three defenders. In view of the placement of the two teams it will be difficult to play an elaborate build-up.
In defense we will have to be very careful of the combinations between the three strikers, but in the attacking plays we can exploit the space which a three-man defense permits us. When a 4-4-2 meets a 3-4-3 the result of the match will probably depend on individual skills and the contests between the single players of the two teams.

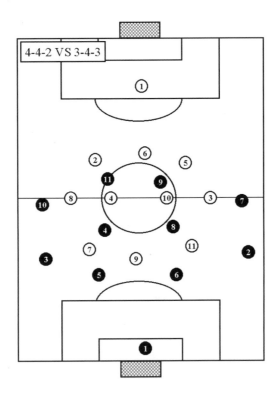

4-4-2 VS 3-4-3

3

THE PRINCIPAL ATTACKING SOLUTIONS OF THE 4–3–3 SYSTEM.

SYSTEM 4-3-3.

The 4-3-3 is a system frequently used in Holland. Dutch soccer is famed and appreciated the world over for the quality of its attacking play and for the many champions that such a small country has succeeded over the years in bringing to the top – due also to the work carried out by the instructors in the training centers for young players. The 4-3-3 allows the team to cover the entire offensive front and gives the players the chance to use their technical ability in attack.

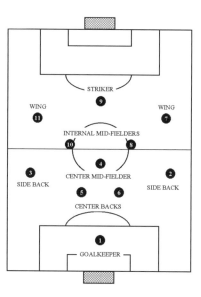

ROLES.
PHYSICAL AND TECHNICAL / TACTICAL STRENGTHS.

SIDE BACKS
• Ability to play with the team in attack both in support and in giving thrust
• Exceptional power, speed and stamina.

- Tactically flexible; able to break into empty spaces.
- Able to keep the defense in line.
- Good with his feet.

CENTER BACKS
- Skills in tackling and in playing in the air.
- Good at long and short passes.
- Able to support the side backs
- Quick at interpreting miscellaneous tactical situations.
- Leadership qualities in his section.
- Exceptional power and speed.

INSIDE MIDFIELDERS
- Excellent physical build and good acceleration.
- Ability to break quickly into open spaces created by the forwards.
- Ability to meet dump and rebound passes from the striker.
- Able to change speed and to give thrust when in possession.
- Good at shooting from far out.
- Constant collaboration in the defense phase.
- Good at tackling and stealing balls.

CENTER MIDFIELDER
- Marked tactical sense.
- Good at shielding the defense
- Excellent technical skills enabling him to manage attacking play and be a permanent point of reference for his teammates.
- Able to help in defense by doubling up on marking

WINGS
- Exceptional technical skills.
- Good at crossing from the sides.
- Good at dribbling.
- Good acceleration.
- Skills in shooting at goal from close up.
- Clear tactical sense. Able to help the defense by directing the opponents' attacking play into a part of the field that will give the greatest possible advantage to his own team.

CENTER STRIKER
- Able to receive and shield a ball.
- Excellent shooting skills with both head and feet – power and precision.
- Mobility.
- Good at creating space for his team-mates.
- Able to use dump and rebound passes to allow for the penetration of the wings or the center midfielders.

THE PLAYS OF THE 4-3-3.

Intensity and organization: playing as a group in build-up.

The team must be able to build up play with confidence, flow and variation. It is important never to lose possession when the team is off balance (too far forward for example) or near or around the area. At the same time, play must be fluid and well-timed. Two-touch plays will help the team to move the ball quickly and give consistency to the operations. The team must also diversify build-up so that the opponents never have clear points of reference. In the following illustrations we will be looking at some examples of how to organize group movements in build-up. We will be able to see how the player can move away from the ball to create space for a teammate coming up to receive it at full speed.

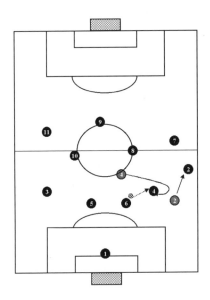

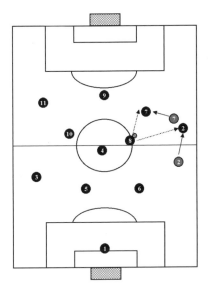

Plays and movements between center midfielder and side back. Center back in possession.

Plays and movements between the wing or the inside midfielder. Center midfielder in possession, with two alternative solutions.

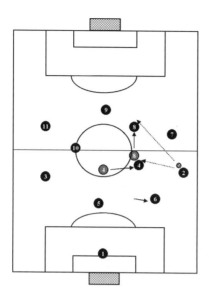

Plays and movements between center and inside midfielders. Side back in possession has two alternative solutions.

BUILD UP WITH A LONG PASS.

We have already looked at the advantages and disadvantages of this tactical play. In the following examples we will be having a look at some ways of building up with a long pass.

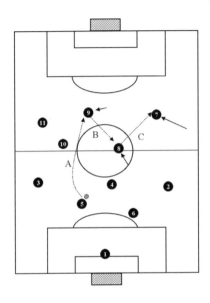

**Immediate build-up:
example I**

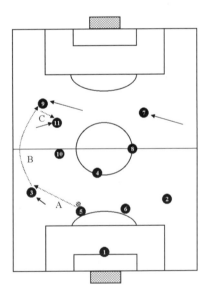

**Immediate build-up:
example 2**

ELABORATE BUILD-UP.
Moving the ball around the defense.

The team must be able to get the ball moving at the back in order
to build up attacking play. In this diagram we can see the chain of
passes and the positions of the backs in a semi-circle or half
moon. The left side back dumps on the left center back who is
behind and diagonally placed to the player in possession. The left
center back then passes to the right center back on the opposite
side of the field. This second pass can only be made if the conditions are completely safe, otherwise he should opt for a long
pass. The right side back will then be able to pass to his teammate on the right, who, having received a diagonal pass will then
be able to take the ball forward.

Moving the ball around the defense.

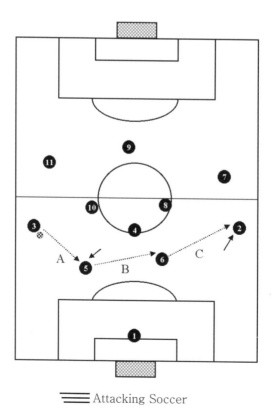

BRINGING THE BALL FORWARD – FROM THE DEFENSIVE THIRD TO THE MIDFIELD BY DIAGONAL PASSES OR PASSES FORWARD FOLLOWED BY A DUMP.

In this sequence we can see how to move the ball up from the defense to the midfield using both diagonal passes and vertical passes followed by a dump.

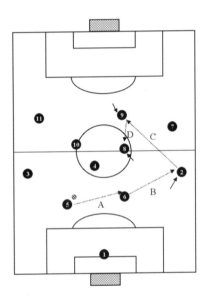

Giving flow by moving the ball up from the defensive third to the midfield.

Giving flow by moving the ball up from the defensive third to the midfield.

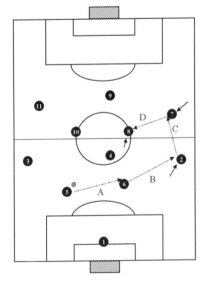

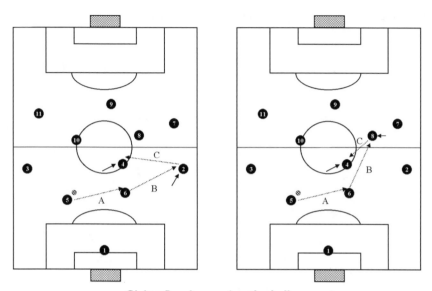

Giving flow by moving the ball up from the defensive third to the midfield.

60

EXAMPLES OF HOW TO BUILD UP PLAY.

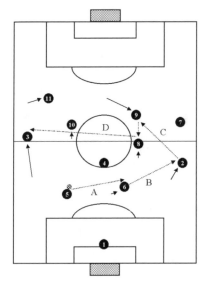

Elaborate build-up: example 1

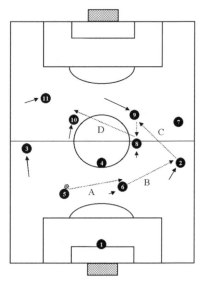

**Elaborate build-up: example 1
1st Alternative**

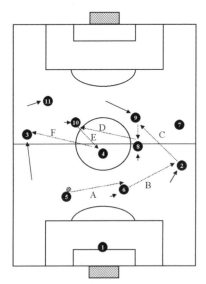

**Elaborate build-up: example 1
2nd Alternative**

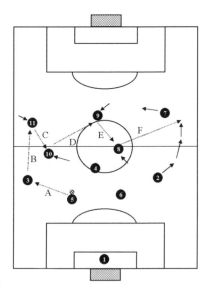

Elaborate build-up: example 2

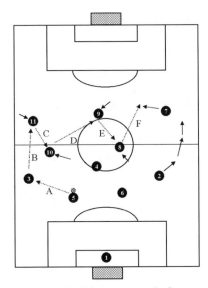

Elaborate build-up: example 2
1st Alternative

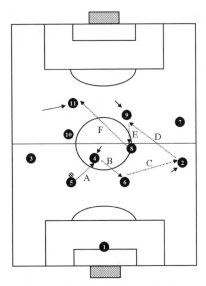

Elaborate build-up: example 3

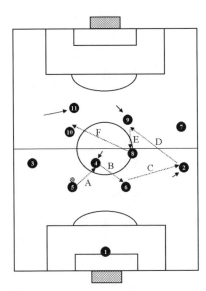

Elaborate build-up: example 3
1st Alternative

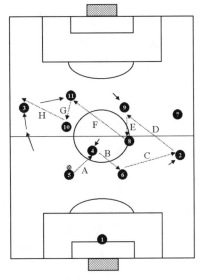

Elaborate-build up: example 3
2nd Alternative

MOBILITY AND ORGANIZATION: COLLECTIVE PLAY IN THE FINISHING TOUCH PHASE.

As we have already seen, the keys to attacking play are confidence, flow and variety. In the finishing touch phase the play must be fast, incisive and appropriate to the opponents' weak points. During finishing touch play it is of the utmost importance that the team moves quickly and in synchrony. In the following figures we will be looking at some examples of collective movements in finishing touch play. Notice how the team frees players from marking by the coordinated movements of two or more players opening up spaces for a teammate to occupy and attack from.

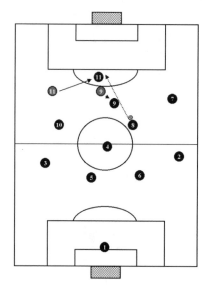 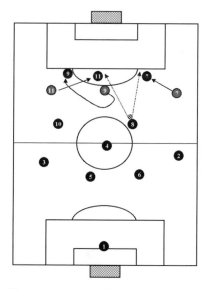

Plays and movements between the wing and the center striker. Inside midfielder in possession.

Plays and movements between the wings and the center striker. Inside midfielder in possession.

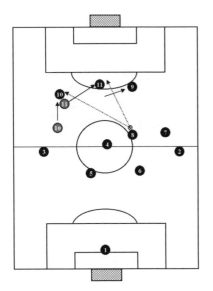

Plays and movements between the center midfielder and the wing. Inside midfielder in possession has two possible solutions.

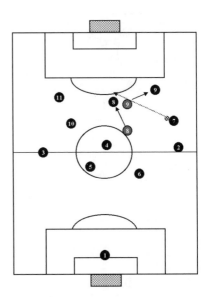

Plays and movements between the center striker and the center midfielder, who comes forward to the space that has been created for him.

64

BREAKS.

A break is when a player steals the ball in his opponents' half. Organized well, this type of play can be very dangerous because the opponents' defense will be unprepared and out of position. When he has gained possession the player must keep the ball and bring it forward a dribble or two in order to give the forwards time to sprint into depth.

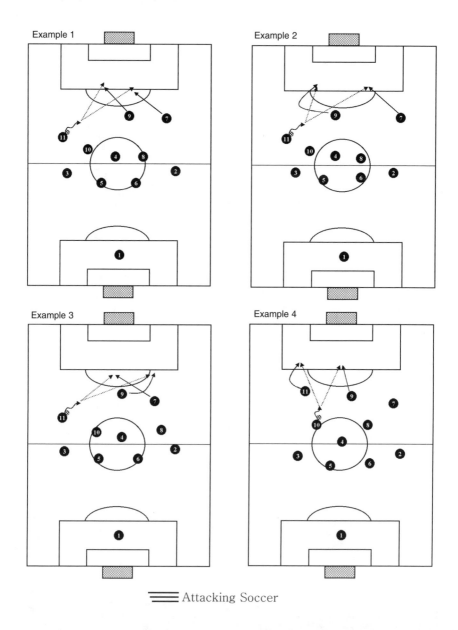

Example 5

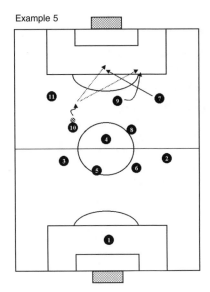

THE ATTACK IN DEPTH.

This attacking play can be developed when the opponents' defense is not too deep. In cases like this the team in possession can attack the space behind the defense using in-depth cuts. In the following illustrations we will see examples of cuts made by players using the 4-3-3 system.

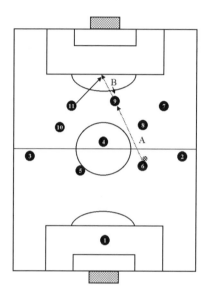

ATTACK IN DEPTH.
Pass (header): center striker to wing.

ATTACK IN DEPTH.
Cut: inside midfielder to wing.

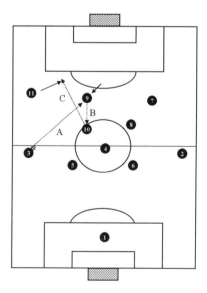

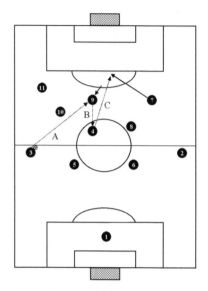

ATTACK IN DEPTH.
Cut: center midfielder to wing.

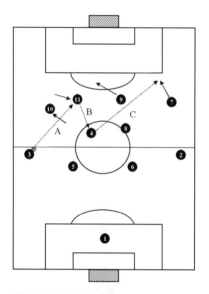

ATTACK IN DEPTH.
Cut: center midfielder to wing.

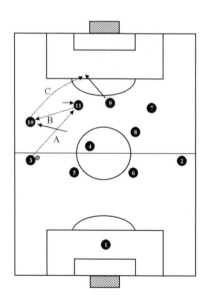

ATTACK IN DEPTH.
Cut: inside midfielder to
center striker.

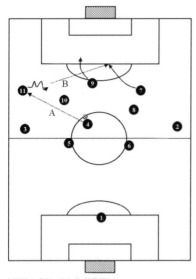

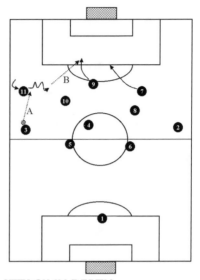

ATTACK IN DEPTH.
Cut: wing to opposite wing.

ATTACK IN DEPTH.
Cut: wing to center striker.

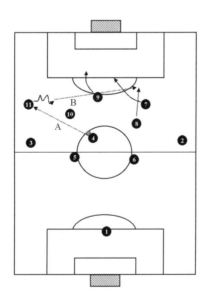

ATTACK IN DEPTH.
Cut: wing to inside midfielder.

SIDE ATTACK.

This type of play is necessary when you must get around a lined up defense on the outside. Overlapping, combinations, dump and rebound passes and cuts are all good ways of getting into position so that you can cross into the area. Here we see some examples of side attacks with the 4-3-3.

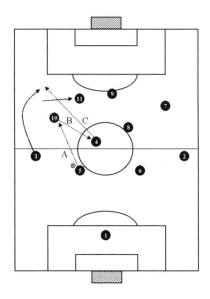

SIDE ATTACK.
Overlapping: center midfielder to side back.

SIDE ATTACK.
Overlapping: inside midfielder to side back.

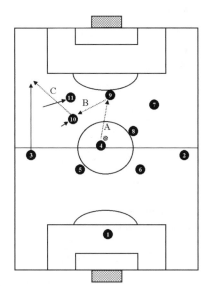

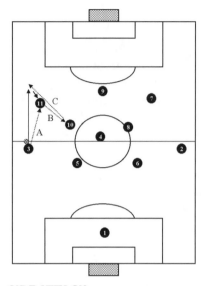

SIDE ATTACK.
Overlapping: inside midfielder to side back.

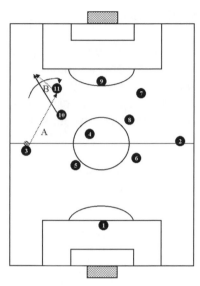

SIDE ATTACK.
Overlapping: wing to inside midfielder.

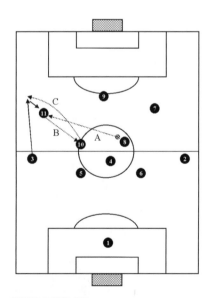

SIDE ATTACK.
Overlapping: inside midfielder to side back.

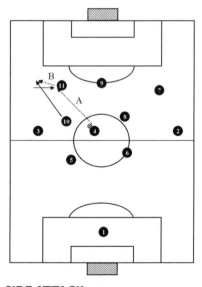

SIDE ATTACK.
Dump and rebound: wing to inside midfielder.

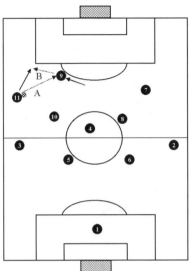

SIDE ATTACK.
Combination: give and go, wing to center striker to wing.

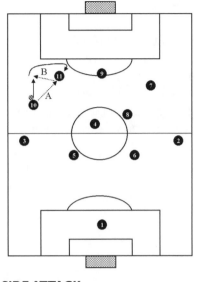

SIDE ATTACK.
Combination: give and go, inside midfielder to wing to inside midfielder.

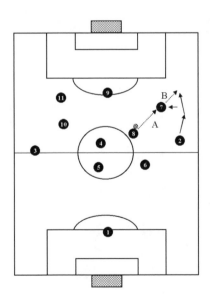

SIDE ATTACK.
Combination: dummy.
Wing makes a dummy, ball goes to side back.

CENTRAL ATTACK.

A drawn up defense line can, however, be attacked by central finishing touches, using dump and rebound passes and combinations. This type of play is generally used as an alternative to side attacks to give variation to the team's play. In the following diagrams we will be showing central plays leading out of dump and rebound passes or combinations.

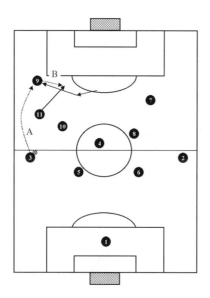

CENTRAL ATTACK.
Dump and rebound: center striker to wing.

CENTRAL ATTACK.
Dump and rebound: center striker to wing.

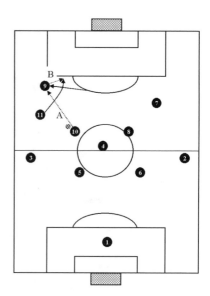

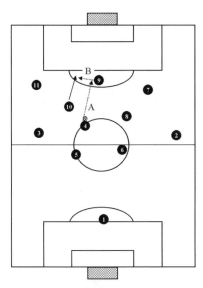

CENTRAL ATTACK.
Dump and rebound: center striker to inside midfielder.

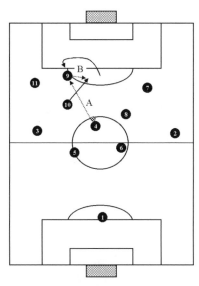

CENTRAL ATTACK.
Dump and rebound: Center striker to inside midfielder.

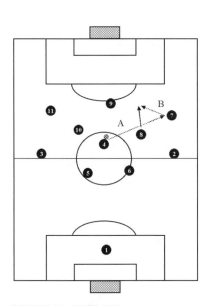

CENTRAL ATTACK.
Dump and rebound: wing to inside midfielder.

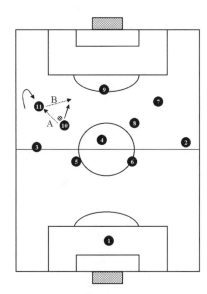

CENTRAL ATTACK.
Combination. give and go, inside midfielder to wing to inside midfielder.

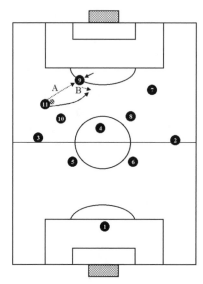

CENTRAL ATTACK.
Combination: give and follow, wing
to center striker to wing.

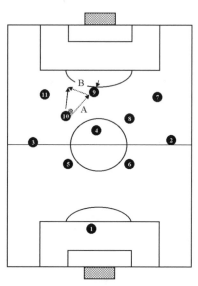

CENTRAL ATTACK.
Combination. give and go, inside
midfielder to center striker to
inside midfielder

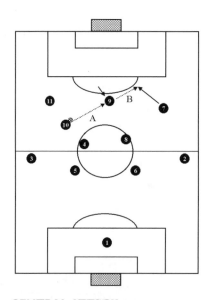

CENTRAL ATTACK.
Combination: dummy.
Center striker makes a dummy,
ball goes to wing.

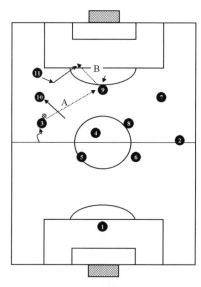

CENTRAL ATTACK.
Dump and rebound: center striker
to wing.

POSITION OF THE PLAYERS FOR A CROSS.

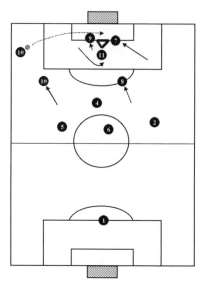

Example I
The center striker closes on the near post,
The opposite wing closes on the far post,
The nearest wing is in the middle,
The left inside midfielder goes in support of
the player in possession,
The right inside midfielder covers the zone
outside the area.

Example 2
The center striker closes on the near post,
The opposite wing closes on the far post,
The right inside midfielder is in the middle,
The left inside midfielder goes in support
of the player in possession,
The center midfielder covers the zone out-
side the area.

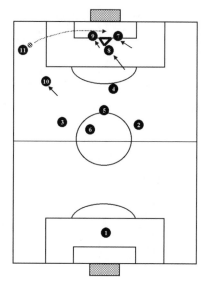

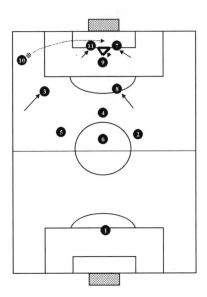

Example 3
The wing closes on the near post,
The opposite wing closes on the far post,
The central striker is in the middle,
The right inside midfielder covers the zone outside the area,
The side back goes up in support.

POSITION WHEN INTERCEPTING A REBOUND.

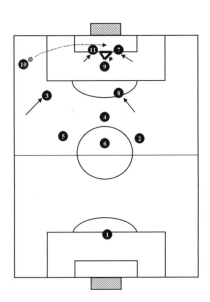

Reaction after intercepting a rebound.

FACING THE OPPONENTS' SYSTEM:

The 4-3-3 against the 3-4-1-2.

In defense, the two strikers and the attacking midfielder of the 3-4-1-2 are met by the center backs and the center midfielder respectively. In defense the side backs should move back in a diagonal direction so that the two strikers do not find themselves in a two against two situation with the center backs.
In attack it is important to utilize the wings, –i.e., the whole attacking front. Remember, the three defense players will be playing three against three and if you play wide they will have more field to cover – which should create more problems for them.

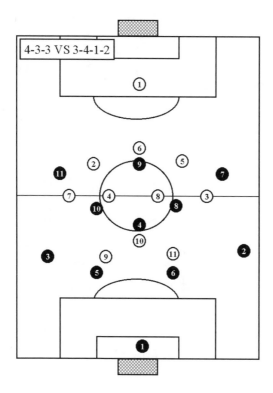

The 4-3-3 against the 3-4-3.

A three man defense is rarely lined up against the wide attacking front of the 4-3-3. What usually happens in these cases is that a side midfielder is brought back to cover the wing with less offensive verve, and a back is placed wide to cover the wing who is stronger in attack.

However, if we have to play against the 3-4-3, remember that we are in numerical superiority in defense (4 backs against 3 strikers), in numerical inferiority in the midfield (3 midfielders against 4) and in a 3 against 3 situation in attack. Depending on our opponents' strength, on the current score and on the tactical situation on the field, we can, (if we are in trouble in the midfield because of our numerical inferiority), try to rectify the situation by:
— moving the side back forward on the flank where the ball is in play;
— moving the wing back on the side not in play.
When we have possession it is important to pass to the wings, who, depending on the distance that separates them from their direct opponent, can stop the ball and try for a one against one situation in depth between the lines.

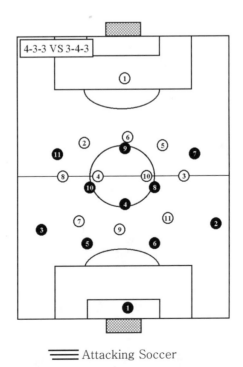

4-3-3 VS 3-4-3

The 4-3-3 against the 3-5-2.

As we have already seen, it rarely happens that a three man defense is lined up to control three forwards when two of these are playing wide. The 3-5-2 will give clear superiority to our opponents' midfield, and this can be contrasted by allowing them to advance so that their side midfielders are deep enough to be controlled by the side backs of the 4-3-3.

When playing against the 3-5-2 it is dangerous to go into offensive pressing because by doing so we would be forced to move our side backs too far forward, leaving the center backs in a two against two situation with the opponents' two strikers. What we should do then, is to give them space, allowing them to come forward. In that case, once we gain possession we can counter attack using the wings and combinations between the forwards.

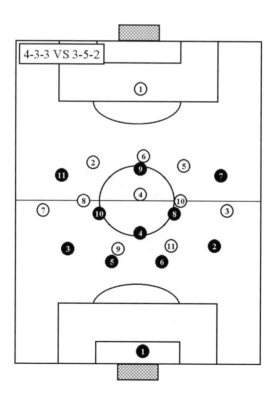

4-3-3 VS 3-5-2

The 4-3-3 against the 4-4-2.

When playing against a team using the 4-4-2 the most important factor is the control of the midfield. Our three midfielders have to face four opponents and will be in difficulty unless they are supported by the side backs. On the other hand, once the 4-3-3 has taken control of the midfield, their in-depth cuts and diagonal passes between the lines to the wings will create serious problems for the opponents.

In defense it is important not to give space to the strikers in order to avoid a 2v2 against the two central defenders.

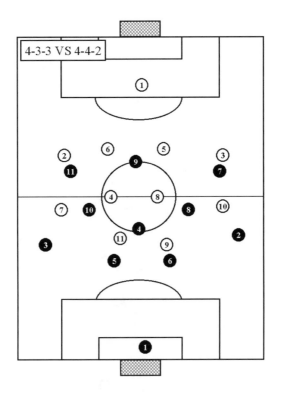

4

THE PRINCIPAL ATTACKING SOLUTIONS OF THE 3-5-2 SYSTEM.

SYSTEM 3-5-2.

In this system, very commonly used in Germany, there are three players in defense, five in the midfield and two strikers. Instead of the four backs that you find in the 4-4-2 and other similar systems, here we have only three players in the defense zone. This gives the team more consistency in the midfield, but it also means that a side midfielder will often have to drop back to cover the flanks. In recent years, in Italy, teams have preferred to use the 3-4-1-2 rather than the 3-5-2 so that players with the necessary technical and tactical skills can operate behind the strikers during finishing touch play.

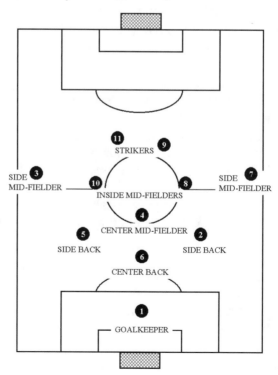

These are the main characteristics necessary in this system:

CENTER BACK.
• Good at covering the entire section, stepping in when his teammates have been beaten or when they are in difficulty.
• Able to pilot the defense division and to keep it near the midfield.
• Good at tackling, good in the air and at contrasting players who try to dribble past him.
• Must play the ball simply, both with short passes and long shots to the strikers.

SIDE BACKS
• Good at marking.
• Able to play wide in order to support attacking moves.
• Must give consistency, coordinating play with the teammates of his division.

CENTER MIDFIELDER
• Good technical skills, allowing him to organize play.
• Tactically intelligent. Able to help the team in defense, placing himself in front of the backs in order to protect them.
• Good at regaining possession and at giving quick direction to the team's play

INSIDE MIDFIELDER
• Exceptional power and stamina.
• Must be able to play without the ball, penetrating whatever spaces he can find.

• Good at shooting from outside the area. Good at passing to teammates moving into attack.

SIDE MIDFIELDER
• All round player: able to attack and defend.
• Good stamina.
• Must go forward into attack and return to cover his flank in defense.
• Precision in crossing.
• Dribbling skills; good at defending against his direct opponent.

STRIKERS
• The strengths of the strikers are more or less those that we have already underlined in looking at the 4-4-2 system.

THE PLAYS OF THE 3-5-2.

Intensity and organization: playing as a group during build up.

The team must be able to build up play with confidence, flow and variation. It is essential not to lose possession when the team is off-balance (in defense, for example) or when the ball is near the penalty box. At the same time, play must be fluid and regulated to perfection. Two-touch play will help to drive the team quickly forward and to give the right tempo to build up. It is important, too, that the team be able to vary their build-up play in order to leave the opponents without points of reference. In the following illustrations we will be having a look at ways of organizing collective play in the build-up phase. In the diagrams we will see how the player near the ball can move away from it, creating space for a teammate moving up to take possession.

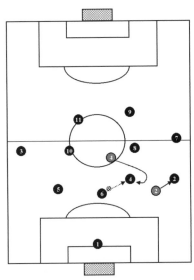 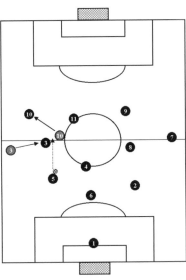

Plays and movements between center midfielder and side back. Center back in possession.

Plays and movements between side and inside midfielders. Side back in possession.

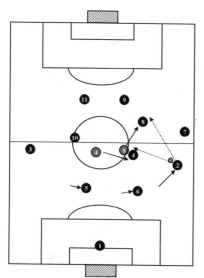

Plays and movements between center and inside midfielders. Side back in possession, has two possible solutions.

BUILDING UP PLAY WITH A LONG PASS.

We have already had a look at the tactical advantages and disadvantages of this way of building up play. Here are a couple examples of building up play by a long pass.

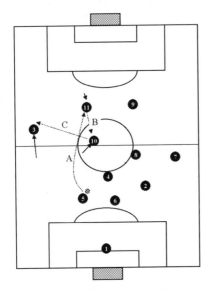

Immediate build-up: example I

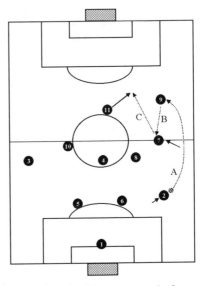

Immediate build-up: example 2

ELABORATE BUILD-UP.

Moving the ball around the defense.

When the defense is in possession the three players of the unit must play wide, spreading themselves out in their established positions on the field. Having only three players in the defense section gives the advantage of being able to use an extra man in front. However, playing with a three man defense system means that each defender will have to cover a wider section of the field. It is extremely important, therefore, that, after gaining possession, the team should be good at keeping the ball on the move and slowing down the pace, giving the side backs time to take up wide positions. If they cannot do so, the team will feel the consequences during build up because the side midfielders will have to move back and we will get a situation of numerical parity or even inequality in the midfield. Keeping the ball on the move between the backs will be much the same with a three- as with a four-man defense system, only, in this case, the center back must be particularly good at supporting the side back in possession.

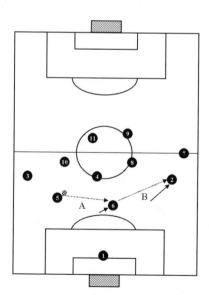

Moving the ball around the defense.

MOVING THE PLAY FORWARD FROM THE DEFENSE TO THE MIDFIELD USING DIAGONAL PASSES OR VERTICAL PASSES FOLLOWED BY A DUMP.

In the following illustrations we will see how to move the ball from the defense to the midfield with diagonal passes or vertical passes followed by a dump.

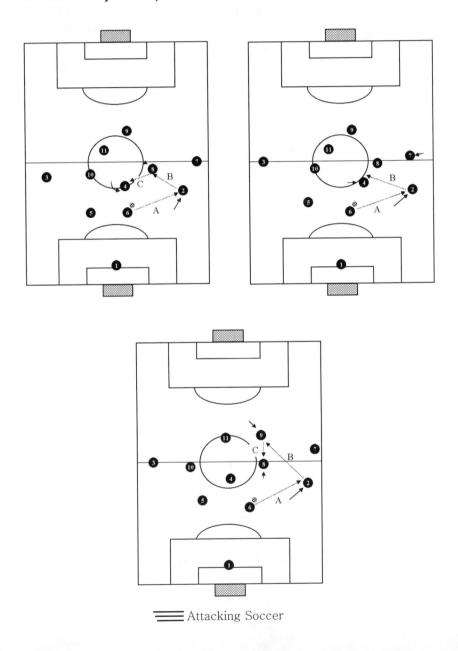

EXAMPLES OF HOW TO BUILD UP PLAY:

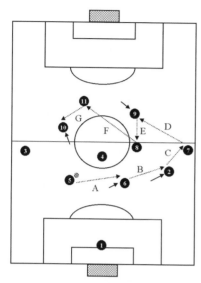

Elaborate build-up: example 1

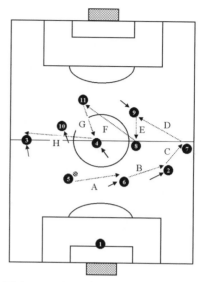

**Elaborate build-up: example 1
1st Alternative**

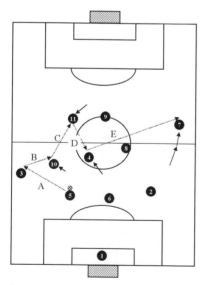

Elaborate build-up: example 2

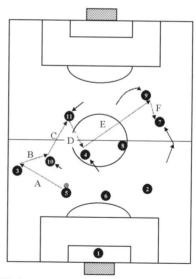

**Elaborate build-up: example 2
1st Alternative**

Attacking Soccer

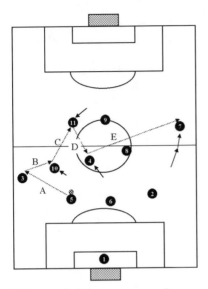

Elaborate build-up: example 3

MOBILITY AND ORGANIZATION: COLLECTIVE PLAY IN THE FINISHING TOUCH PHASE.

We have already seen that the principle characteristics of attacking play are confidence, flow and variety. During finishing touches, play must be quick and sharp. Speed and timing are essential, and it is important also to attack our opponents' weakest points. In the following illustrations we will be looking at some examples of collective play in finishing touch play. Note how the joint action of two or more players can free a teammate of marking: by moving together they disengage a part of the field, creating space for another player to attack.

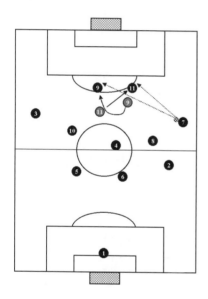

Plays and movements between the two strikers. Inside midfielder in possession can pass to either striker.

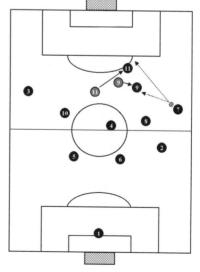

Plays and movements between the two strikers. Inside midfielder in possession.

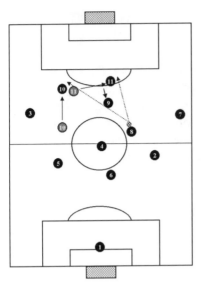

Plays and movements between a striker and an inside midfielder. The other inside midfielder in possession can pass to either teammate.

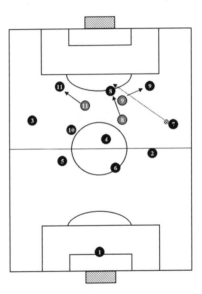

Plays and movements between the strikers (creating space) and the inside midfielder (breaking into the space that has been created for him).

BREAKS

A break is when a player steals the ball in his opponents' half. This type of play can be very dangerous because the opponents' defense will be unprepared and out of position. Having stolen the ball, the player in possession should keep it for a dribble or two in order to give the strikers time to sprint into depth.

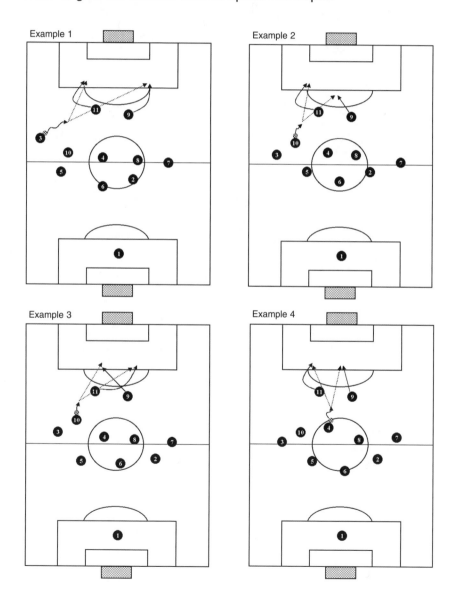

Example 1

Example 2

Example 3

Example 4

Example 5

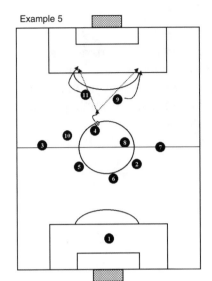

Example 6

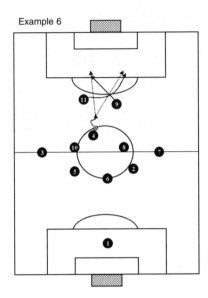

THE ATTACK IN DEPTH.

This type of attacking play develops when the opponents'
defense section is high. In situations like this the team in possession can attack the space behind the defense line using in-depth
cuts. In the following illustrations we will be looking at cuts made
by players using the 3-5-2 system.

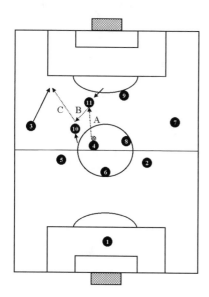

ATTACK IN DEPTH.
Cut: inside to side midfielder.

ATTACK IN DEPTH.
Cut: center midfielder to striker.

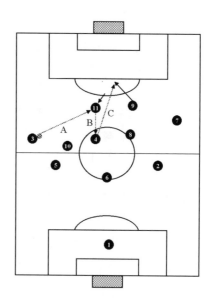

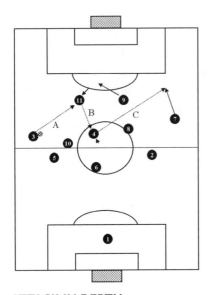

ATTACK IN DEPTH.
Cut: center to side midfielder.

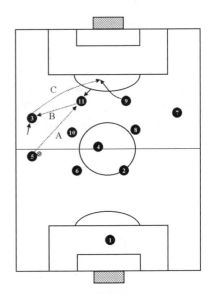

ATTACK IN DEPTH.
Cut: side midfielder to striker.

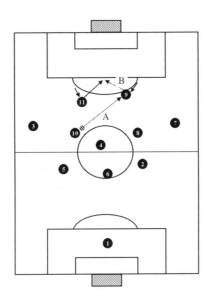

ATTACK IN DEPTH.
Dump and rebound: left to right striker.

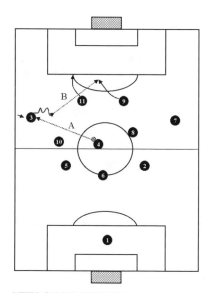

ATTACK IN DEPTH.
Cut: side midfielder to striker.

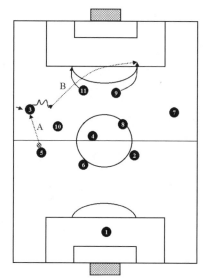

ATTACK IN DEPTH.
Cut: side midfielder to striker.

SIDE ATTACK.

This type of play is necessary when you must get around a lined up defense on the outside. Overlapping, combinations, dump and rebound passes and cuts are all good ways of getting into position so that you can cross into the area. Here we see some examples of side attacks with the 3-5-2.

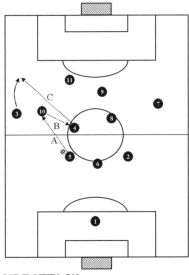

SIDE ATTACK
Overlapping: center to left side midfielder.

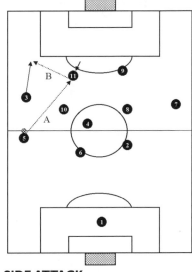

SIDE ATTACK.
Dump and rebound: striker to side midfielder.

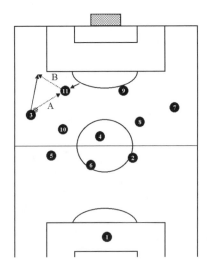

SIDE ATTACK
Combination: give and go.
Side midfielder to striker to side midfielder.

CENTRAL ATTACK.

A drawn up defense line can, however, be attacked by central finishing touches, using dump and rebound passes and combinations. This type of play is generally used as an alternative to side
attacks to give variation to the team's play. In the following diagrams we will be showing central plays leading out of dump and
rebound passes or combinations.

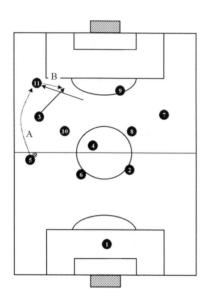

CENTRAL ATTACK
**Dump and rebound: striker to
side midfielder.**

CENTRAL ATTACK
**Dump and rebound: striker
to side midfielder.**

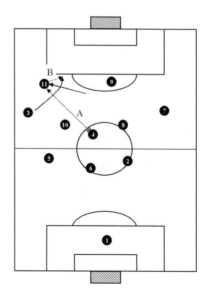

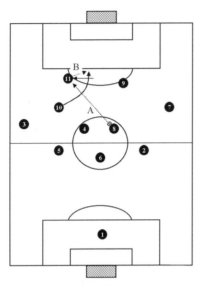

CENTRAL ATTACK
Dump and rebound: striker to inside midfielder.

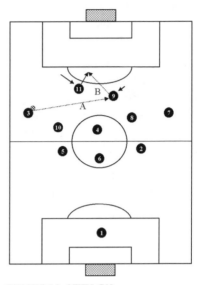

CENTRAL ATTACK
Dump and rebound: right to left striker.

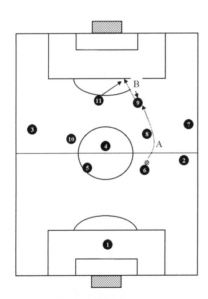

CENTRAL ATTACK
Dump and rebound. right to left striker.

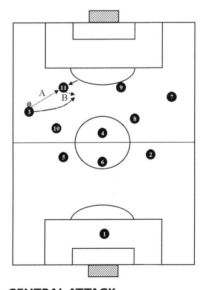

CENTRAL ATTACK
Combination: give and follow.
Side midfielder to striker to side midfielder.

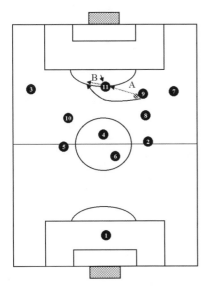

CENTRAL ATTACK.
Combination: give and follow.
striker to striker to striker.

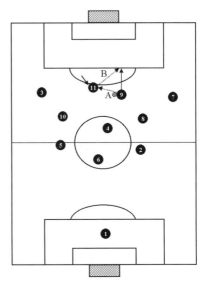

CENTRAL ATTACK.
Combination: give and go.
striker to striker to striker.

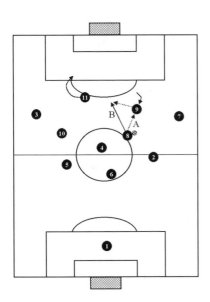

CENTRAL ATTACK
Combination: give and go.
Inside midfielder to striker to
inside midfielder.

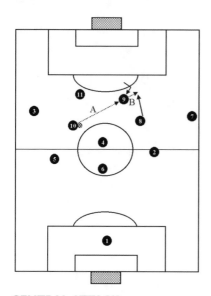

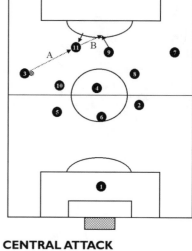

CENTRAL ATTACK
Combination: dummy.
Striker makes a dummy; ball goes to inside midfielder.

CENTRAL ATTACK
Combination: dummy.
Striker makes a dummy; ball goes to a teammate in attack.

POSITION OF THE PLAYERS FOR A CROSS.

This is how the players should place themselves to receive a cross:

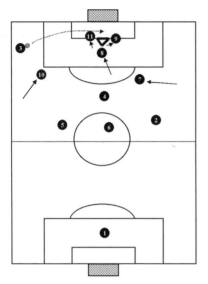

Example 1.
The two strikers cover the area around the two posts.
The right inside midfielder breaks into the center.
The side midfielder on the opposite side of the field from where the cross is kicked comes up to the limit of the area.
The other inside midfielder supports the player in possession.

Example 2.
The two strikers cover the central area and the near post.
The side midfielder on the opposite side of the field from where the cross is kicked places himself near the far post.
One of the inside midfielders comes up to the limit of the area, while the other supports the player in possession.

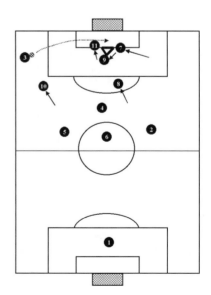

POSITION WHEN INTERCEPTING A REBOUND.

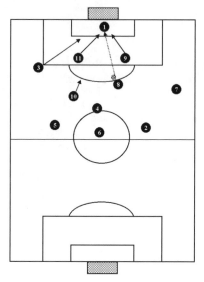

How to cover the rebound area after shooting at goal.

FACING THE OPPONENTS' SYSTEM:

The 3-5-2 against the 3-4-1-2.

When playing against the 3-4-1-2 we must watch the attacking midfielder very carefully. He can be marked in two ways:
– by moving the center midfielder back a few yards;
– by moving the center back forwards a few yards.
If we go for the first option, we will have to do without a midfielder, but we keep numerical superiority in defense. If we select the second, we will have the same numbers in defense but numerical superiority in the midfield. Obviously, before making our choice, we will have to consider factors like:
– our opponents' individual and the all round strengths;
– the physical condition of the two teams
– the particular tactical moment of the match, based on the
  ongoing result.

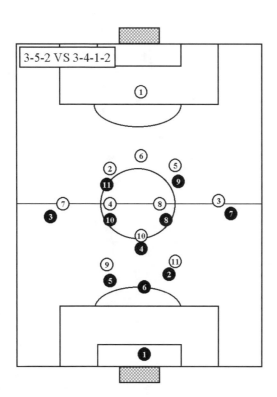

3-5-2 VS 3-4-1-2

The 3-5-2 against the 3-4-3.

Strikers using the 3-4-3 play nearer to each other than in the 4-3-3, so we will normally have numerical parity in defense (three backs against three strikers). This will be all right as long as our team is carrying the play and the defense is in control. In the midfield, the center midfielder must use his liberty to set up attacking play. In attack, our two strikers have to face three backs and they will have to play in close cohesion to create goal scoring situations.

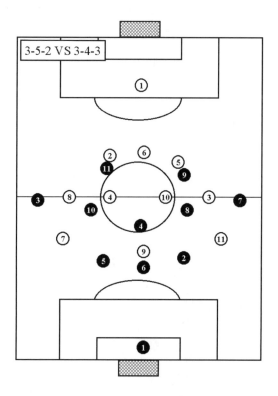

The 3-5-2 against the 3-5-2.

When two teams both using the 3-5-2 face each other, the first thing to notice is that the defense plays in numerical superiority while in the number of midfielders is the same. The team that controls play will probably win. Organization, the physical condition of the players and the ability of the midfielders – these are the things that are likely to make the difference.

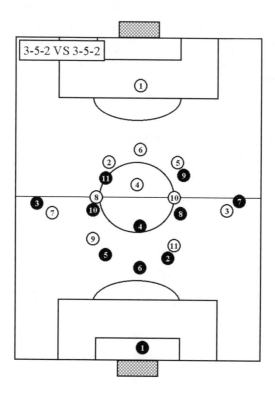

The 3-5-2 against the 4-3-3.

When playing against a team with the wings lined up wide, we can adjust the 3-5-2 in the following ways:
– a side midfielder can be brought back to cover one of the wings;
– a back can be placed wide to cover the other.
By moving players around in such a way, the three-man defense turns itself into a four-man defense.
We can also stick to the 3-5-2 system by moving the side midfielders back. They will have to mark the wings on the side of the field where the ball is not in play. If you want to play like this, however, the team must be able to time things well and the players must be skilled at moving back at the right moment.
Having regained possession it is important to exploit our numerical superiority in the midfield: whenever he can, one or other of the side midfielders must move up into attack.

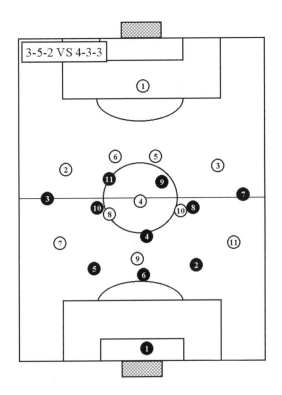

3-5-2 VS 4-3-3

The 3-5-2 against the 4-4-2.

Tactically speaking, this will be an even match. The fact that we have 5 midfielders against our opponents' 4 will not give us a great advantage, simply because a team playing with the 4-4-2 can bring one or the other side defenders up to balance the situation when the ball is in play on his side. The 3-5-2 has only one side player (as against the two of the 4-4-2); but this is not a problem either, because an inside midfielder can be brought back to stabilize the tactical standing of the teams. The winner will probably be the team with the highest technical standards, the greatest ability in moving back in time and the best physical condition – independently of the system they are using.

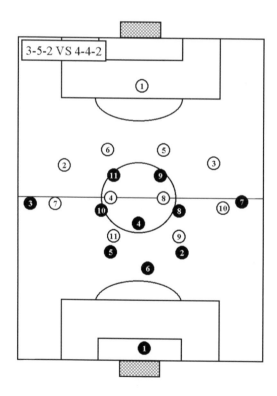

3-5-2 VS 4-4-2

5

THE PRINCIPAL ATTACKING SOLUTIONS OF THE 4-3-1-2 SYSTEM.

SYSTEM 4-3-1-2.

The 4-3-1-2 puts an attacking midfielder behind the two strikers. This playing system is a more offensive variant of the 4-4-2. In the 4-4-2, the four midfielders are placed in line; whereas in the 4-3-1-2 they are positioned in the form of the 'rhombus', with a low end and an attacking edge.

Let us now have a detailed look at the particular strong points of the players in the various roles.

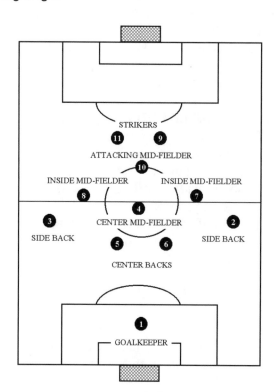

ROLES
PHYSICAL AND TECHNICAL \ TACTICAL STRENGTHS.

CENTER BACK.
- Good defensive ability.
- Able to conduct the defense.
- Tactically intelligent; able to foresee the opponents' play.
- Technical skills.

SIDE BACKS.
- Able to move up in attack.
- Even better in defense.
- Good sprinting and stamina.
- Able to interpret tactical situations, collaborating with his teammates in defense.

CENTER MIDFIELDERS.
- High standard in blocking players and tackling.
- Able to direct attacking play quickly and with tactical intelligence.
- Good at organizing pressing.

INSIDE MIDFIELDERS.
- Stamina: non-stop running.
- Must be clear-headed: able to defend and attack.
- Good at tackling and at timing his moves into attack
- Good at shooting from a distance.
- Able to cooperate with the other midfielders.

ATTACKING MIDFIELDER
- Excellent technical strengths.
- Able to pass in depth to teammates.
- Excellent tactical intelligence: must be able to develop the team's

attacking play with timing and by
giving ideal direction to the ball.
• Fairly good participation in defense.

STRIKERS.

The two strikers must be compatible, of course. The particular
strengths of one must also fill out the other's.

So if one is:
• able to protect the ball
• good with his head and physically
  powerful
• strong in the area and good at creating space

Then his companion should be:
• always in motion and very quick
• good at dribbling and able to play
  with imagination
• good at shooting from a distance.

Players like this will give the team all the finishing touches necessary to make attacking play as varied and unpredictable as possible.

THE PLAYS OF THE 3-5-2.

Intensity and organization: playing as a group in build up.

The team must be able to build up play with confidence, flow and variation. It is essential not to lose possession when the team is off-balance (in defense, for example) or when the ball is near the penalty box. At the same time, play must be fluid and regulated to perfection. Two-touch play will help to drive the team quickly forward and to give the right tempo to build up. It is important, too, that the team be able to vary their build-up play in order to leave the opponents without points of reference. In the following illustrations we will be having a look at ways of organizing collective play in the build up phase. In the diagrams we will see how the player near the ball can move away from it, creating space for a teammate moving up to take possession.

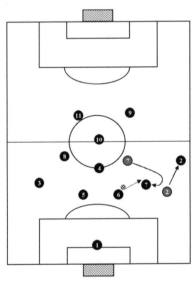

Plays and movements between the inside midfielder and the side back. Center back in possession.

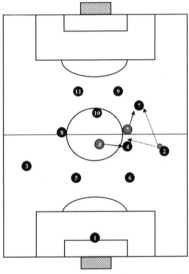

Plays and movements between the center and inside midfielder. Side back in possession has two possible solutions.

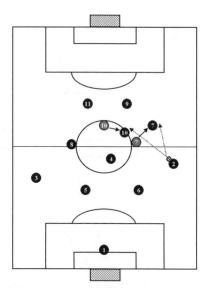

**Plays and movements between the
inside and the attacking midfielder.
Side back in possession, with two
possible solutions.**

BUILDING UP PLAY WITH A LONG PASS.

We have already had a look at the tactical advantages and disadvantages of this way of building up play. Here are some examples of building up play by a long pass.

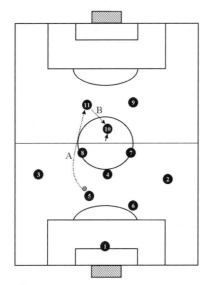

Immediate build-up: example I

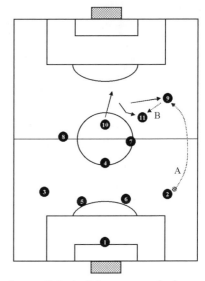

Immediate build-up: example I

ELABORATE BUILD-UP.
Moving the ball around the defense.

It is all important that the team manages to keep the ball on the move among the backs so as to build up a well ordered attack. In the illustration below we can see the linked passes and the placement of the backs in a semicircle or half moon. First of all, the left side defender dumps the ball on the left center back who is behind and placed diagonally to him. The left center back then passes in the opposite direction to the right center back; of course, if he cannot do this in complete safety, then he should go for a long pass. Having gained possession, the right center back can then pass up to the right side back, who after receiving a diagonal pass will be able to move the ball ahead.

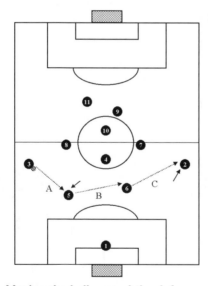

Moving the ball around the defense.

BRINGING THE BALL FORWARD - FROM THE DEFENSIVE THIRD TO THE MIDFIELD BY DIAGONAL PASSES OR PASSES FORWARD FOLLOWED BY A DUMP.

In the following illustrations we will see how to move the ball from the defense to the midfield with diagonal passes or vertical passes followed by a dump.

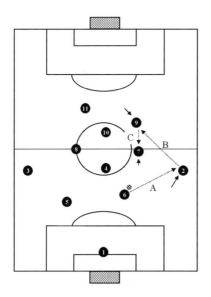

Giving flow by moving the ball up from the defensive third to the midfield.

Giving flow by moving the ball up from the defensive third to the midfield.

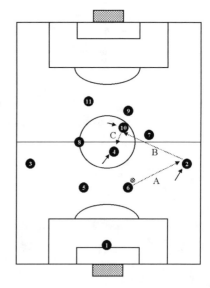

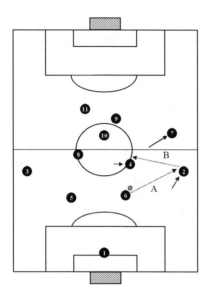

Giving flow by moving the ball up from the defensive third to the midfield.

Giving flow by moving the ball up from the defensive third to the midfield.

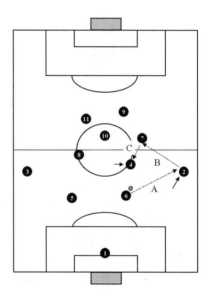

SOME EXAMPLES OF PLAY DURING BUILD-UP.

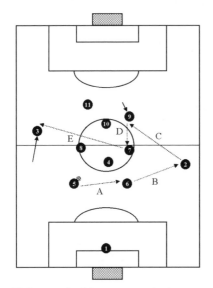

Elaborate build-up: example 1

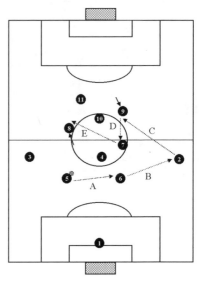

**Elaborate build-up: example 1
1st Alternative**

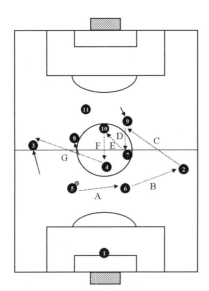

**Elaborate build-up: example 1
2nd Alternative**

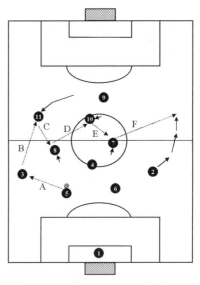

Elaborate build-up: example 2

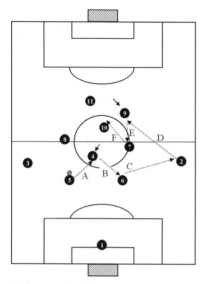

Elaborate build-up: example 3

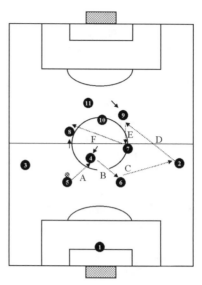

**Elaborate build-up: example 3
1st Alternative**

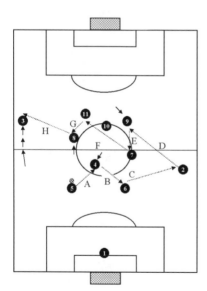

**Elaborate build-up: example 3
2nd Alternative**

MOBILITY AND ORGANIZATION: COLLECTIVE PLAY IN THE FINISHING TOUCH PHASE.

We have already seen that the principle characteristics of attacking play are confidence, flow and variety. During finishing touches, play must be quick and sharp. Speed and timing are essential, and it is important also to attack our opponents' weakest points. In the following illustrations we will be looking at some examples of collective play during finishing touches. Note how the joint action of two or more players can free a teammate of marking: by moving together they disengage a part of the field; moving into this, another player can then attack from there.

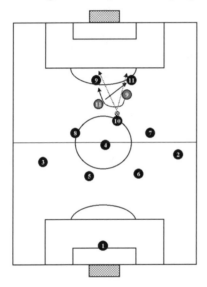 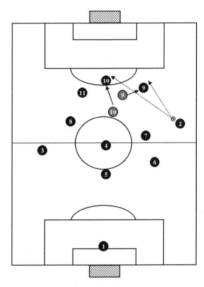

Plays and movements between the two strikers. Attacking midfielder in possession can pass to either of the strikers.

Plays and movements between a striker and the attacking midfielder. Side back in possession.

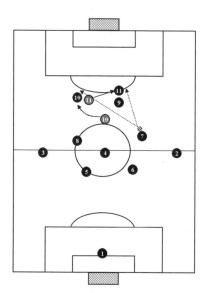 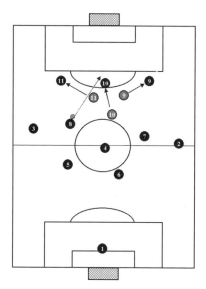

Plays and movements between a striker and the attacking midfielder. Inside midfielder in possession can pass to either teammate.

Plays and movements between the strikers and the attacking midfielder breaking into the central space that has been opened up.

BREAKS

A break is when a player steals the ball in his opponents' half. Organized well, this type of play can be very dangerous because the opponents' defense will be unprepared and out of position. When he has gained possession, the player must keep the ball and bring it forward a dribble or two in order to give the strikers time to sprint into depth.

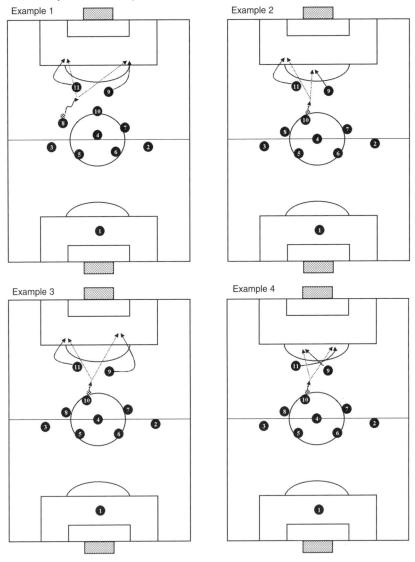

THE ATTACK IN DEPTH.

This type of attacking play develops when the opponents' defense section is high. In situations like this the team in possession can attack the space behind the defense line using in-depth cuts. In the following illustrations we will be looking at cuts made by players playing in the 4-3-1-2 system.

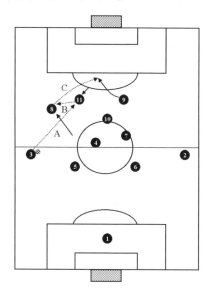

ATTACK IN DEPTH
Cut: inside midfielder to striker.

ATTACK IN DEPTH
Cut: Attacking midfielder to striker.

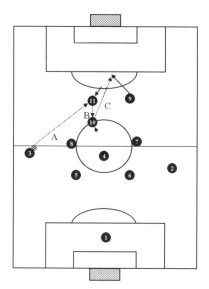

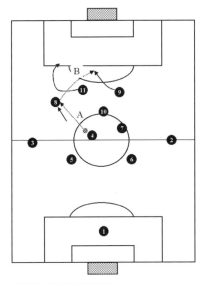

ATTACK IN DEPTH
Cut: inside midfielder to striker.

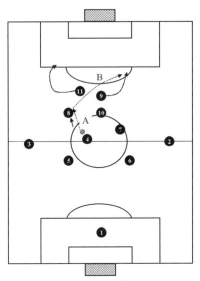

ATTACK IN DEPTH
Cut: inside midfielder to striker.

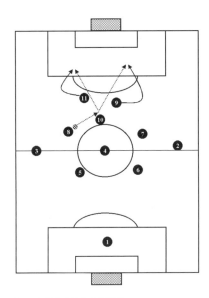

ATTACK IN DEPTH
Cut: attacking midfielder to striker.

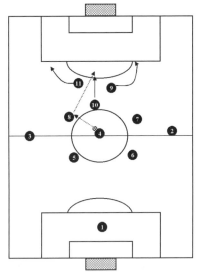

ATTACK IN DEPTH
Cut: side to attacking midfielder.

SIDE ATTACK.

This type of play is necessary when you must get around a lined up defense on the outside. Overlapping, combinations, dump and rebound passes and cuts are all good ways of getting into position so that you can cross into the area. Here we see some examples of side attacks with the 4-3-1-2.

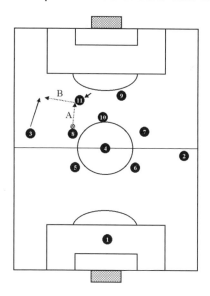

SIDE ATTACK
Dump and rebound: striker to side back.

SIDE ATTACK
Combination: give and go.
Side back to striker to side back.

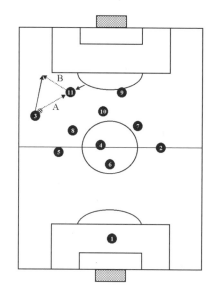

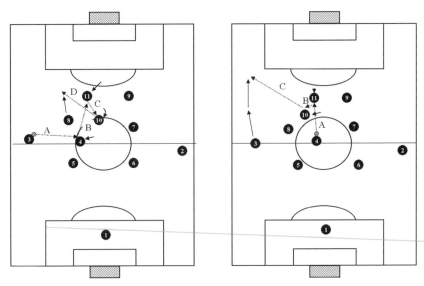

SIDE ATTACK
Cut: attacking to center midfielder.

SIDE ATTACK
Cut: attacking midfielder to side back.

CENTRAL ATTACK.

A drawn up defense line can, however, be attacked by central finishing touches, using dump and rebound passes and combinations. This type of play is generally used as an alternative to side attacks to give variation to the team's play. In the following diagrams we will be showing central plays leading out of dump and rebound passes or combinations.

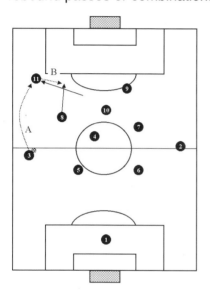

CENTRAL ATTACK
Dump and rebound: striker to inside midfielder.

CENTRAL ATTACK
Dump and rebound: striker to inside midfielder.

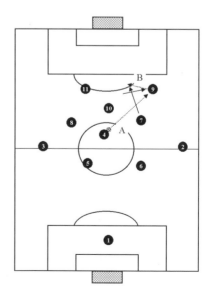

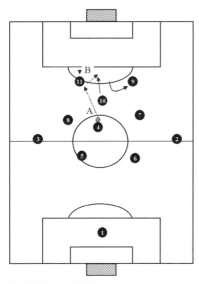

CENTRAL ATTACK
Dump and rebound: striker to
attacking midfielder.

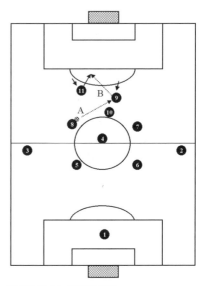

CENTRAL ATTACK
Dump and rebound. right to left
striker.

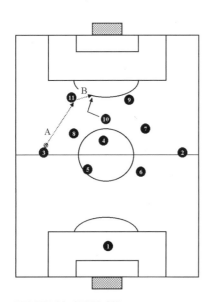

CENTRAL ATTACK
Dump and rebound: striker to
attacking midfielder.

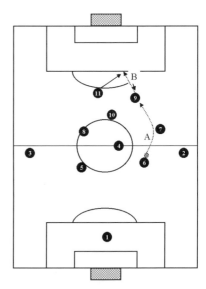

CENTRAL ATTACK
Dump and rebound. right to left
striker.

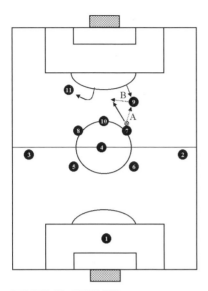

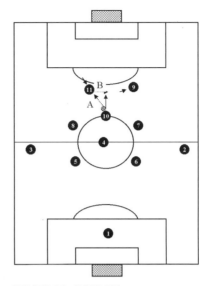

CENTRAL ATTACK
Combination: give and follow.
Inside midfielder to striker to
inside midfielder.

CENTRAL ATTACK
Combination: give and go.
attacking midfielder to striker to
attacking midfielder

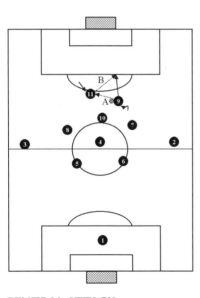

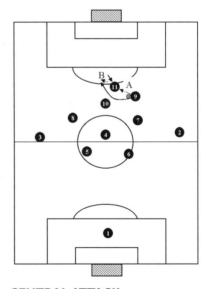

CENTRAL ATTACK
Combination: give and go.
Striker to striker to striker.

CENTRAL ATTACK
Combination: give and follow.
Striker to striker to striker.

Attacking Soccer

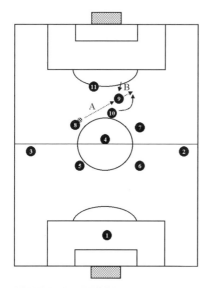

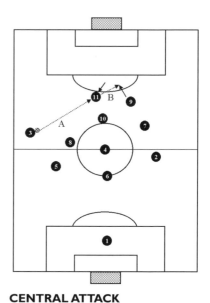

CENTRAL ATTACK
Combination: dummy.
Striker makes a dummy, ball goes to attacking midfielder.

CENTRAL ATTACK
Combination: dummy.
Left striker makes a dummy in the middle, ball goes to his teammate in the same role.

POSITION OF THE PLAYERS FOR A CROSS.

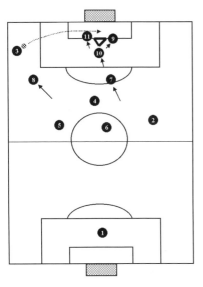

Example I:
the two strikers cover the area between the posts;
the attacking midfielder breaks into the center;
the inside midfielder on the other side of the field places himself at the edge of the area;
the other inside midfielder supports the player in possession.

Example 2:
the attacking midfielder is ready for the cross;
the two strikers cover the area around the posts;
the inside midfielder on the other side of the field places himself in the center;
the other inside midfielder is at the edge of the area;
the side back supports the player in possession.

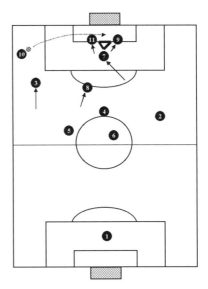

POSITION WHEN INTERCEPTING A REBOUND.

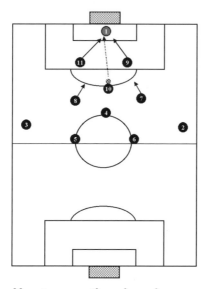

**How to cover the rebound area
after a shot on goal.**

FACING THE OPPONENTS' SYSTEM.

The 4-3-1-2 against the 3-4-1-2.

In the defense phase the two strikers and the attacking midfielder of the 3-4-1-2 are controlled by the center backs and the center midfielder respectively. The two side backs must close in diagonally so that the two strikers are not playing in a two on two situation with the center backs.
In attack we must use the side backs to set up play and to create a two against one situation (side back and inside midfielder against the side backs of the 3-4-1-2) and so create effective side attacks.

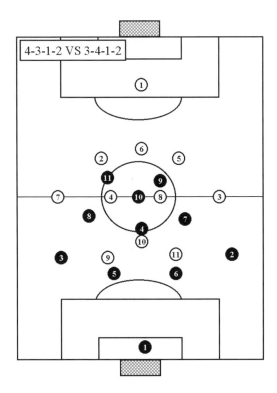

4-3-1-2 VS 3-4-1-2

The 4-3-1-2 against the 3-4-3.

An opponent using the 3-4-3 might make it difficult for us to exploit our side backs' attacking play. We must take as much advantage as we can of our inside midfielders: placed half way between the opponents' side and center midfielders they will have space. When the 4-3-1-2 plays against the 3-4-3 both teams have 4 players in the midfield but the defense players in the first have numerical superiority over the attacking players of the other. In any case, it will be a balanced match and, physical fitness permitting, the team with the better organization will probably come out victorious.

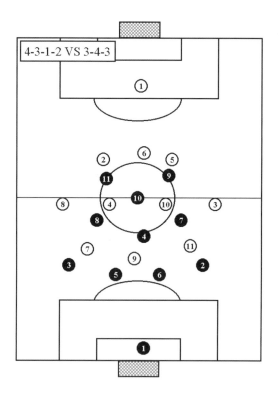

The 4-3-1-2 against the 3-5-2.

When playing against the 3-5-2 the most important thing is to confine our opponents' numerical superiority in the midfield. We can resolve this problem by advancing the side back when the ball is in play in his section so that he covers his opponents' side midfielder. In-depth pressing is difficult when playing with the 4-3-1-2 because it would be a mistake to bring the side backs into advanced positions. In the center, the attacking midfielder could go into offensive pressing with the support of the inside midfielders ready to cover the opponents' dumps – and this would be effective, though difficult to carry out.

When our team is in possession against the 3-5-2 it is easy enough to control play, passing the ball to the side backs or the center midfielder. Freeing players so that they can shoot will not be so straightforward, however, because it goes without saying that our opponents will be marking the strikers and the inside and attacking midfielders.

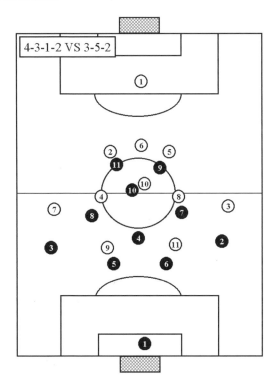

The 4-3-1-2 against the 4-4-2.

Both teams have a four-man defense playing against two strikers. It will come naturally to the two sides to pass the ball to the side backs, who will have more space to play in. When the team is in possession, the attacking midfielder should play between the lines, for this will create more problems for the opponents. When not in possession (or in the defense phase) the attacking midfielder should block the opponents' center midfielder, otherwise the team will come under too much pressure in the midfield. Also, our team's inside midfielders should be ready to move wide in order to obstruct their opponents' midfielders or side backs – depending on the kind of pressing the team wishes to play. When the inside midfielder moves wide the side backs must move up in support.

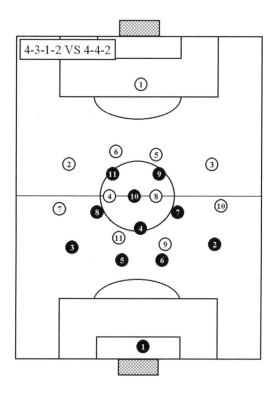

4-3-1-2 VS 4-4-2

6

THE PRINCIPAL ATTACKING SOLUTIONS OF THE 4-5-1 SYSTEM.

SYSTEM 4-5-1.

The 4-5-1 is more widely used than you would think in modern soccer. Coaches like to have numerical superiority in the center of the field and will not hesitate to bring back the striker, changing the 4-4-2 into a 4-4-1-1 (which is, in fact, a 4-5-1), or putting the wings of the 4-3-3 at the same level as the midfielders so that they have a five-man unit. The main risk run by a team using the 4-5-1 is to turn defense into an obsession. If the players do not have a good attacking mentality and do not go forward to shoot at goal, they may end up by losing control of the play.

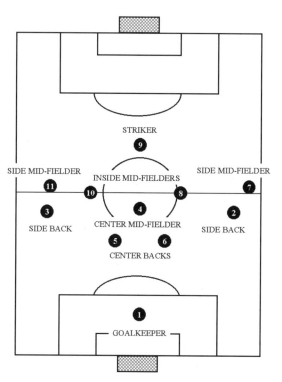

Let us have a detailed look at the main strengths of the players who use the 4-5-1.

ROLES
PHYSICAL AND TECHNICAL \ TACTICAL STRENGTHS.

CENTER BACKS
- Excellent ability in defense
- Good with his head. Good at tackling.
- Knows how to take up the best position in relation to his opponents' attacking plays.
- Able to cover his teammates in defense.
- Good tempo: able to move in collaboration with his teammates in defense.
- Good technical level: able to lead play when the conditions are right.

SIDE BACKS.
- Good ability to close up space in defense. Good at playing with his teammates in defense.
- Able to support attacking play.
- Good at running. Good stamina.

CENTER MIDFIELDER
- Good ability both at interrupting the opponents' play and at giving thrust to his own team in his turn.
- Able to position himself in the best possible way in collaboration with his teammates.
- Able to guide his teammates in pressing.
- Good at doubling up on marking.

INSIDE MIDFIELDERS.
- Excellent athletic strength, clinching this players ability to play a decisive role both in attack and defense.
- Excellent tempo; able to move with intelligence without the ball.
- Able to score goals; good at giving assists to his teammates.

SIDE MIDFIELDERS.
- Naturally offensive in play.
- Fast and with good stamina: must be able to run up and down along the sidelines.
- Able to cross, and give in-depth assists.
- Complete perception of what the nearest inside midfielder and the striker are doing. Must be able to understand their play.

STRIKER.
- Excellent protection of the ball.
- Able to hold his section by himself, giving his teammates time to come up in support.
- Good with his head; good at dump and rebound passes.
- Intelligent tactically; good at creating space for his teammates.
- Accurate in shooting

THE PLAYS OF THE 4-5-1.

Intensity and organization: playing as a group in build up.

The team must be able to build up play with confidence, flow and variation. It is essential not to lose possession when the team is off-balance (in defense, for example) or when the ball is near the penalty box. At the same time, play must be fluid and regulated to perfection. Two touch play will help to drive the team quickly forward and to give the right tempo to build up. It is important, too, that the team be able to vary their build-up play in order to leave the opponents without points of reference. In the following illustrations we will be having a look at ways of organizing collective play in the build-up phase. In the diagrams we will see how the player near the ball can move away from it, creating space for a teammate moving up to take possession.

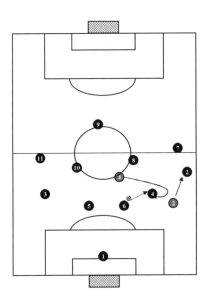

Plays and movements between the center midfielder and the side back. Center back in possession.

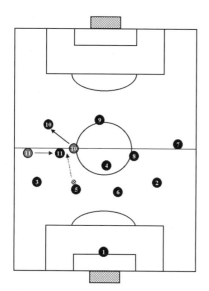 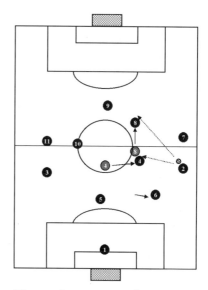

Plays and movements between
the side and inside midfielder.
Center back in possession.

Plays and movements between
the center and inside midfielder .
Side back in possession has two
possible solutions.

BUILDING UP PLAY WITH A LONG PASS.

We have already had a look at the tactical advantages and disadvantages of this way of building up play. Here are some examples of building up play by a long pass. It is not easy playing with the 4-5-1 to build up play with long passes, unless, of course the striker is very good at dominating high balls and at using dump and rebound passes.

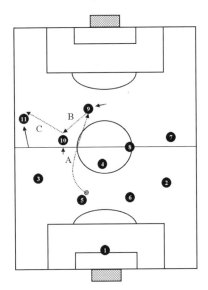

Immediate build-up: example 1

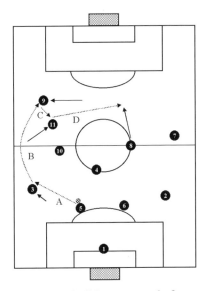

Immediate build-up: example 2

ELABORATE BUILD-UP.
Moving the ball around the defense.

It is vital that the team should 'move the ball behind' in order to
set up attacking play. In this diagram we see the ideal placement
of the players in a semicircle or half moon and their interconnected passes. In the first pass the left side-back dumps the ball to
the center side back who is behind and placed diagonally to the
player in possession. The left side-back then passes to the right
side-back, i.e., opening up the line of play. If he is not sure that
he can do this he should opt instead for a long pass. Once he
has possession, the right side-back can pass to a player to his
right who, having received the pass, will be in a good position to
move play forward.

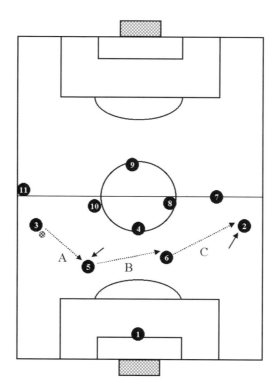

Moving the ball around the defense.

MOVING THE BALL FORWARD FROM THE DEFENSE TO THE MIDFIELD USING DIAGONAL PASSES OR VERTICAL PASSES FOLLOWED BY A DUMP.

In the following illustrations we will see how to move the ball from the defense to the midfield with diagonal passes or vertical passes followed by a dump.

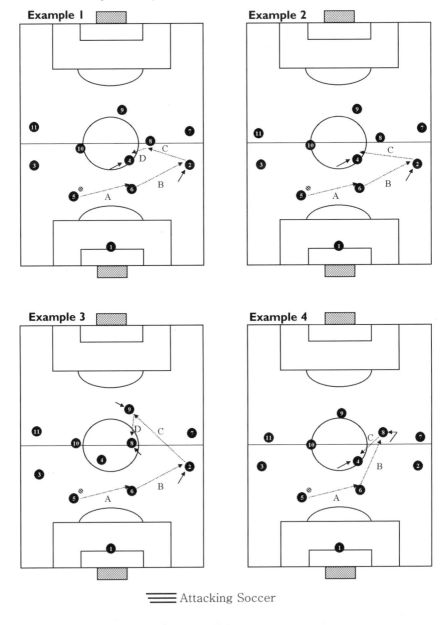

EXAMPLES OF HOW TO BUILD UP PLAY:

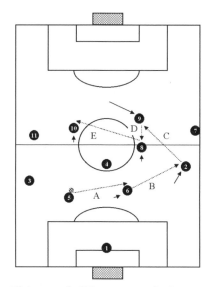

Elaborate build-up: example 1

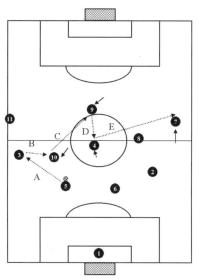

Elaborate build-up: example 2

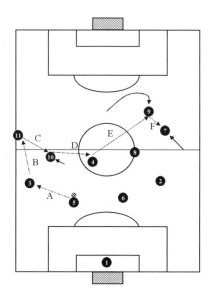

**Elaborate build-up: example 2
1st Alternative**

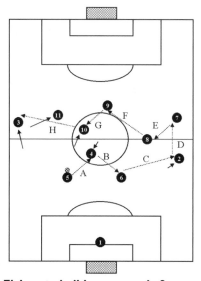

Elaborate build-up: example 3

MOBILITY AND ORGANIZATION: COLLECTIVE PLAY IN THE FINISHING TOUCH PHASE.

We have already seen that the principle characteristics of attacking play are confidence, flow and variety. During finishing touches, play must be quick and sharp. Speed and timing are essential, and it is important also to attack our opponents' weakest points. In the following illustrations we will be looking at some examples of collective play in finishing touch play. Note how the joint action of two or more players can free a teammate of marking: by moving together they disengage a part of the field; moving into this, another player can attack from there.

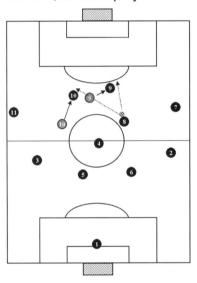

Plays and movements between the striker and the inside midfielder. The other inside midfielder in possession can pass to either teammate.

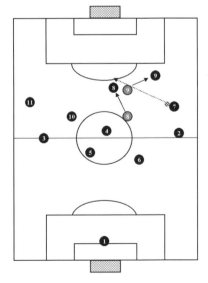

Plays and movements between the striker and the inside midfielder breaking into the space created for him.

BREAKS

A break is when a player steals the ball in his opponents' half. Organized well, this type of play can be very dangerous because the opponents' defense will be unprepared and out of position. When he has gained possession, the player must keep the ball and bring it forward a meter or two in order to give the strikers time to sprint into depth.

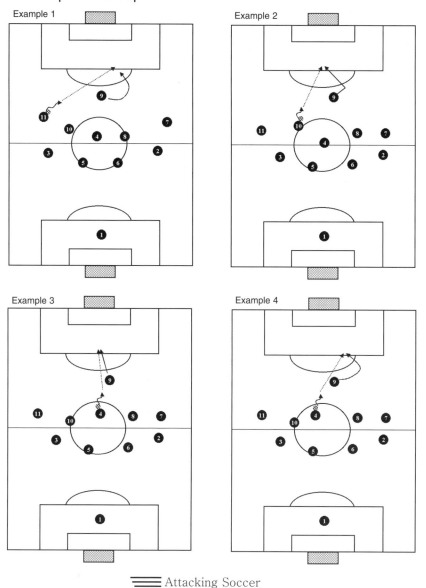

THE ATTACK IN DEPTH.

This type of attacking play develops when the opponents' defense section is high. In situations like this the team in possession can attack the space behind the defense line using in depth cuts. In the following illustrations we will be looking at cuts made by players using the 4-5-1 system.

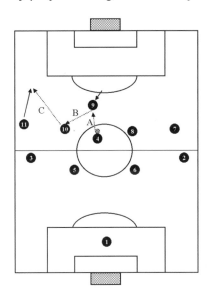

ATTACK IN DEPTH.
Cut: inside to side midfielders.

ATTACK IN DEPTH
Cut: center to side midfielder.

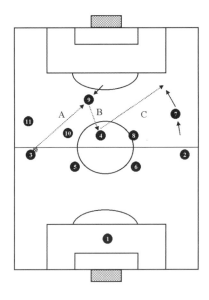

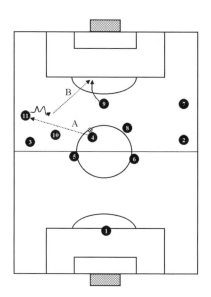

ATTACK IN DEPTH
Cut: side midfielder to striker.

ATTACK IN DEPTH
Cut: side midfielder to striker.

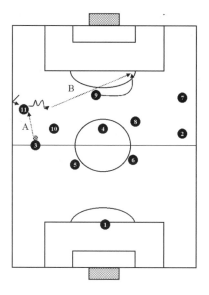

SIDE ATTACK.

This type of play is necessary when you must get around a lined up defense on the outside. Overlapping, combinations, dump and rebound passes and cuts are all good ways of getting into position so that you can cross into the area. Here we see some examples of side attacks with the 4-5-1.

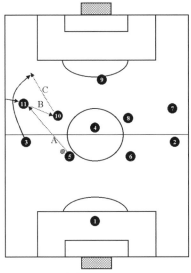

SIDE ATTACK
Overlapping: center to left side midfielder.

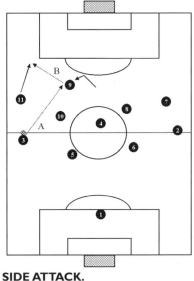

SIDE ATTACK.
Dump and rebound: striker to side midfielder.

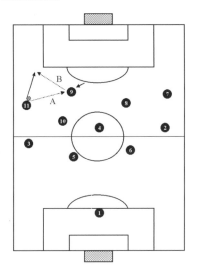

SIDE ATTACK
Combination: give and go. Side midfielder to striker to side midfielder.

CENTRAL ATTACK.

A drawn up defense line can, however, be attacked by central finishing touches, using dump and rebound passes and combinations. This type of play is generally used as an alternative to side
attacks to give variation to the team's play. In the following diagrams we will be showing central plays leading out of dump and
rebound passes or combinations.

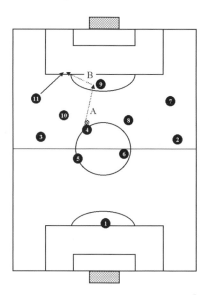

CENTRAL ATTACK
**Dump and rebound: striker to
side midfielder.**

CENTRAL ATTACK
**Dump and rebound: striker
to inside midfielder.**

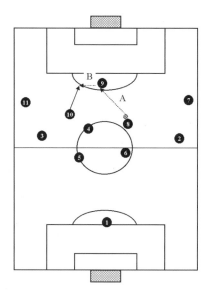

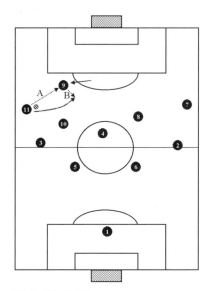

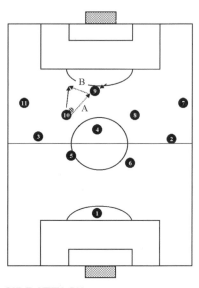

SIDE ATTACK
Combination: give and follow.
Side midfielder to striker to side midfielder.

SIDE ATTACK
Combination. give and go.
Inside midfielder to striker to inside midfielder.

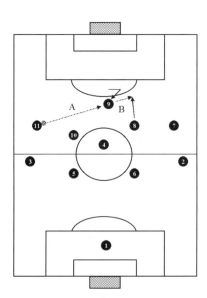

SIDE ATTACK
Combination. dummy.
Striker makes a dummy, ball goes to inside midfielder.

POSITION OF THE PLAYERS FOR A CROSS.

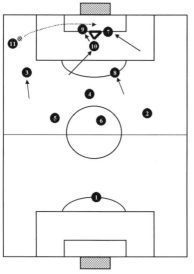

Example 1:
The center striker is on the near post;
The inside midfielder breaks into the middle;
The side midfielder playing on the opposite side of the field is on the far post;
The left inside midfielder goes out of the area.

Example 2:
The center striker is on the far post;
The side midfielder on the opposite side of the field puts himself outside the area;
One of the inside midfielders (the No. 8 in this example) is in the middle of the area; the other (No. 10) is on the near post.

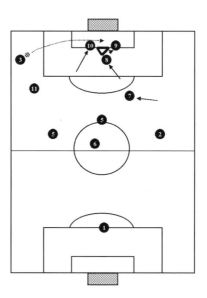

POSITION WHEN INTERCEPTING A REBOUND.

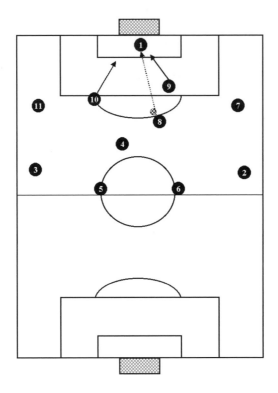

How to cover the rebound area after shooting at goal.

FACING THE OPPONENTS' SYSTEM.

The 4-5-1 against the 3-4-1-2.

Clearly, the 4-5-1 is a defensive system. The players must be good at keeping possession and at pressing, otherwise the pressure will prove too much for them.

Indeed, ball possession is the most important thing, giving the team the chance to control the field of play, and to attack with the greater number of men so that the single center striker is not too isolated. Playing against the 3-4-1-2 means bringing the side back in, so that there is never numerical parity in the center. The attacking midfielder will be contained by the center midfielder with the other midfielders holding on to the opponents' four-man midfield sector. In the attacking phase we will have to rely on

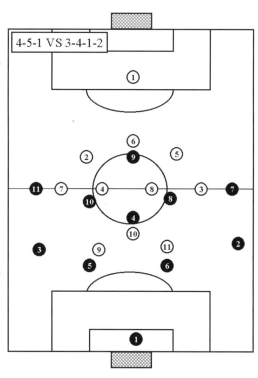

4-5-1 VS 3-4-1-2

the work and movement of the side backs. They will be important points of reference during build-up, and their movements will often create numerical superiority on the sidelines. The four midfielders will be able to break into open space following on dump and rebound passes from the striker, and this is a another move that can be used in situations where our team has possession.

The 4-5-1 against the 3-4-3.

The four backs of the 4-5-1 are a good barrier against the three strikers of the 3-4-3. In addition, the 4-5-1 has numerical superiority in the midfield. Against this, however, so as not to leave the initiative in our opponents' hands, the 4-5-1 must keep up continuous and effective pressing, which will block the other team's play, and allow our players to put them under pressure when they have regained possession.

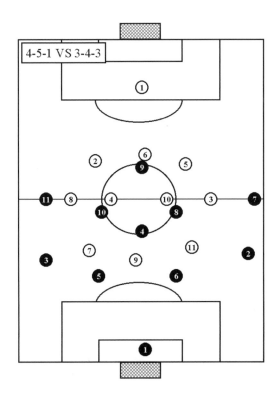

The 4-5-1 against the 3-5-2.

Both teams have five players in the midfield, and so a lot will depend on individual confrontation. Both center midfielders will be free to move because they are not involved in the direct control of any of their opponents, and will be able, therefore, to dedicate all their energies to the build-up phase. Both defense sections are playing in numerical superiority and both teams can play the ball on the sides during build-up. The side with the strongest midfield will probably come out on top.

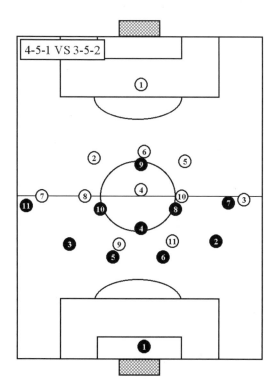

The 4-5-1 against the 4-3-3.

As we have already seen, a four-man defense system can easily contain three strikers. In the midfield the three midfielders of the 4-3-3 will be covered by the three center midfielders of the 4-5-1, while the side midfielders must be ready to arrest the progression of our opponents' side backs. Our team will have to press well and counter attack rapidly to apply pressure.

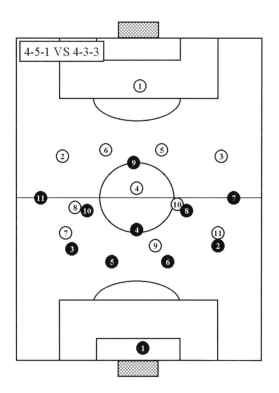

The 4-5-1 against the 4-4-2.

Using the 4-5-1 it is possible to contain a team that plays with the 4-4-2. The side midfielders of the 4-5-1 must be ready to move up and come out to meet the opponents' side backs. In the same way either the midfield can play wide or the side backs can move up to stop the opponents' side midfielders when they go into attack. As we have already seen, pressing must be effective so that the team can keep its balance and does not allow the opponents to sink it too far back into its own midfield.

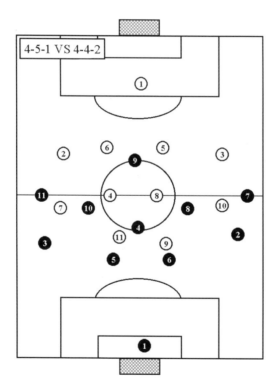

TRAINING THE ATTACKING PHASE

TRAINING THE ATTACKING PHASE.

There is no point at all in a coach being an authority from a technical or a tactical point of view if he is not able to get his ideas across to his team using the right teaching methods.
His ability to communicate must therefore be on a level with his know-how.

If an attacking play is to have success the players must have the right technical \ tactical preparation and the plays themselves must develop out of an overall context that will guarantee their success.

Exercises that teach the attacking phase must stimulate:

1) the individual abilities of each player
2) the abilities of each single section or of the team as a whole in resolving tactical problems connected with the various sub phases of the attacking phase.
3) the comprehension and implementation of the strategy and the collective plays arranged by the coach and connected to the system of play.

INDIVIDUAL EXERCISES.

If we consider the tactical situation of a team in the attacking phase (i.e., when it is in possession), we will see at once that the player in possession can:

1) kick the ball (pass it or shoot at goal);
2) keep possession (dribbling or moving forward).

At the same time, one or more of his teammates, who are not in possession but are preparing themselves to develop the attacking play, must be able to:

1) free themselves of marking;
2) control the ball that they have just received;
3) defend it from the opponents' pressure.

From the point of view of the individual, the main abilities that the coach will have to train are the following:
• passing the ball;
• shooting at goal;
• dribbling an opponent;
• moving forward with the ball;
• getting free of marking;
• receiving and controlling the ball;
• defending the ball.

It is a good idea in training to begin with the easiest exercises, moving on up to the more complicated ones. The simplest exercises aim to fix the particular motory skills required by each technical movement, and these are called exercises in basic technique. The next step is to introduce exercises that call for those same movements, but this time under differing conditions. These second kind of exercises are called applied technique. At the top level, the player will be asked to carry out a particular technical movement in association or as a result of achieving certain individual tactical aims.

EXERCISES TO IMPROVE PASSING TECHNIQUES.

- Two players are inside a delimited area. They pass the ball to each other using various parts of the foot, constantly changing the distance that separates them as they move around the space.

- Two players pass the ball to each other, trying not to hit the cones (diag. 287).

This exercise helps the players to practice passing balls to players as they are running.

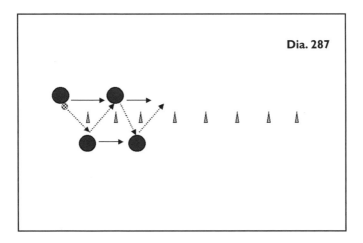

Dia. 287

- In a delimited area, the players placed at the corners pass the ball to a teammate in the center. They vary the direction of the pass – sending it directly to him or into open space. The player in the center, by moving or remaining immobile, will determine the direction of the pass. When the player in the center has received the ball he will dump it back on the teammate who passed it to him, after which he will go to receive another ball from another teammate. The players at the corners will get practice in passing the ball directly to a player or passing into open space where he will be able to run up and receive it. The player in the center practices passing the ball as he is in movement and varying the length of the pass. After a fixed time, the players change places. (diagram 288)

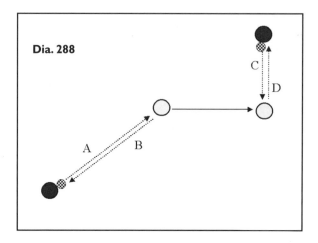

• Pairs of players are chosen, and they have to pass the ball to each other in the group, taking care not to hit the other players involved in the exercise. (diagram 289)

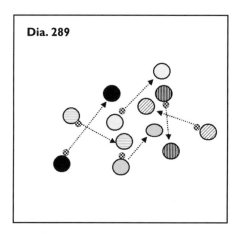

EXERCISES TO IMPROVE TECHNIQUES TO GET FREE FROM MARKING

• Inside a triangular area three pairs of players are involved in an exercise, each pair with a different colored vest (i.e., 2 red, 2 green and 2 yellow). They must keep moving all the time and keep passing the ball to each other following this rule: the player in possession can pass only to a teammate whose vest is a different color from his and is not the same color as the one worn by the player who passed the ball to him in the first place. When the coach gives the signal the player in possession will gain a point for his team if he passes to a teammate whose vest is the same color as his and who has freed himself from marking in the rectangles placed outside the triangle. After a fixed time the players inside the triangle will change places and roles. (diagram 290)

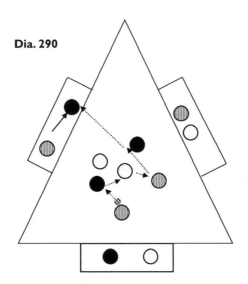

Dia. 290

• Two teams of eight players face each other in a
rectangle. Before the exercise begins the coach will
have chosen pairs of players who must mark each other
as in the diagram, and who can anticipate only the player who has been assigned to them. Each team gets a
point whenever it can carry out a predetermined number
of passes (5, for example) without the opponent having
intercepted the ball. To help the player in possession,
especially if you are training young players, you can
also introduce a special rule saying that the man marking the player in possession must always give his opponent three seconds to play before putting pressure on
him. In that way, it becomes very important for a player
to free himself of marking if he wants to score a point.
(diagram 291)

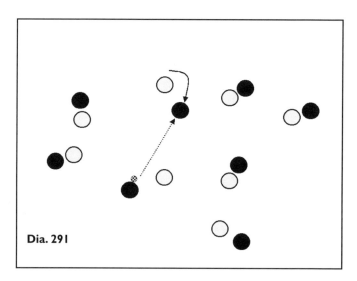

Dia. 291

The following exercise is good for teaching side players how to free themselves of marking.

- Two players pass the ball to each other at the center of the work area. At a sign from the coach (or at their own discretion), the player in possession begins to run towards the player situated near the sideline, who, by freeing himself of marking, prepares to receive the ball. To get free of the player marking him this second player can run towards the baseline or diagonally into the interior of the field (diagram 292). Clearly, the back will have to try to stop his opponent from receiving the pass and he will gain a point every time he manages to intercept the ball. The side players will gain a point for their team when they have correctly received the pass. After a fixed period, it might be a good idea for the players to change roles.

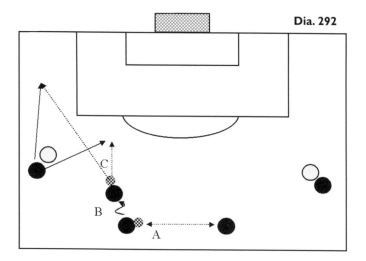

Dia. 292

EXERCISES FOR IMPROVING BALL CONTROL.

- In pairs: a player kicks, giving various trajectories to the ball, and the other receives using various parts of his feet or body.

- In pairs: a player passes the ball to his teammate and then runs off towards a prearranged place on the field while the second is stopping the ball in such a way as to continue running with the ball towards the same area. This exercise is very important for improving receptions that allow the player to continue in the desired direction.

- In pairs in crowded situations: in a fixed area all the pairs have to carry out the previous exercise, taking care that they don't come in contact or bump into each other.

EXERCISES FOR IMPROVING BALL DEFENSE TECHNIQUES.

- In pairs: a player punts the ball a couple of times, and then kicks it high. The other controls the ball and then defends it from an attack by the first.

- Two players pass the ball to each other inside a rectangular or a square area. At a signal from the coach the player in possession has to defend the ball from his teammate's attack.

- Three players with different colored vests pass each other the ball inside an area. The coach whistles, shouting at the same time one of the three colors, and the player wearing the vest of that color must go and attack the player in possession. If the player of that same color happens to be in possession, then the other two players of the group go and attack him. After a second or two the coach signals again and the players restart the exercise. (diagram 293)

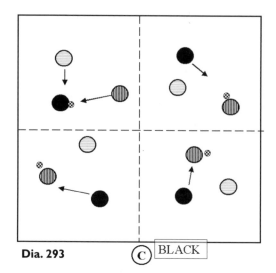

Dia. 293   Ⓒ BLACK

EXERCISES FOR IMPROVING TECHNIQUES OF RUNNING WITH THE BALL.

- In pairs: one of the two is in possession while the other is free to move about in the delimited area. The player with the ball must steer the ball as he follows his team-mate's movements.

- This exercise has the same set up as the last, with the difference that all the pairs are now asked to work in the same area in crowded conditions. When the coach signals and indicates a particular zone of the area the players in possession must take the ball to that zone. At the same time, players without the ball must go to the opposite zone. (diagram 294)

Dia. 294

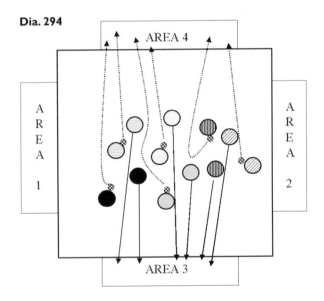

• This exercise takes place in a field divided into three sectors. In each sector two players per team face each other. The coach throws the ball high into the central sector. The player in the central sector who gains possession must bring the ball quickly forward into the attacking sector in order to create numerical superiority there and to try to shoot at goal with the help of his teammates. The players in the central zone who have not managed to gain possession can not oppose the player in possession who is moving towards the attacking zone. On the contrary, this job falls to a player from his team's attacking sector, who will have to move quickly back. The play ends with a shot at goal or with the defending team regaining possession. The exercise then starts again as before with the coach who throws the ball into the central sector where the players have returned to their original places. At a certain point it would be possible for the players to change sectors. (diagram 295)

Dia. 295

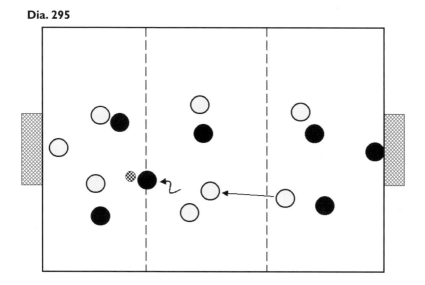

174

EXERCISES FOR IMPROVING DRIBBLING.

• The player in possession carries out a slalom between cones at maximum speed. This is a fundamental exercise to give a sense of how to control the ball at speed and with changes of direction. (diagram 296)

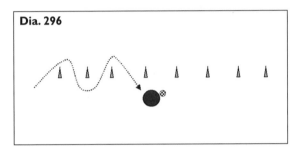

Dia. 296

• In pairs: two players pass each other the ball inside a rectangle. When the coach gives the sign the player in possession will have to bring the ball behind the other player without going out of the rectangle. (diagram 297)

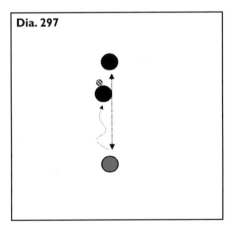

Dia. 297

• Two teams of 6-8 players are occupying a playing field as in the diagram, i.e., with half the players in the attacking zone and the other half in defense. Each player has a direct opponent to get by if he is a striker; to control if he is a back. The purpose of the exercise is to train the strikers' ability at dribbling past the defense. What happens is this: the coach gives the ball to one of the backs, who, because he can not go over the dividing line of the field, will have to pass it to one of his strikers moving around in the attacking zone in the attempt to get free of marking. When the striker has received the ball, not being able to count on his teammates' help, he will have to shoot at goal, trying to get round his direct opponent. If the back regains possession, he will be forced to pass as quickly as he can to his strikers before he is tackled by his opposite number. (diagram 298)

Dia. 298

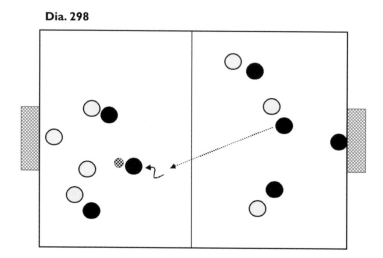

EXERCISES FOR IMPROVING SHOOTING TECHNIQUES.

• A number of balls are positioned at the very limit of the area, and a player shoots these towards the goal. As soon as he has kicked each ball the player has to run quickly round the cone placed outside the area and go to kick another ball as shown in the diagram. (diagram 299)

Dia. 299

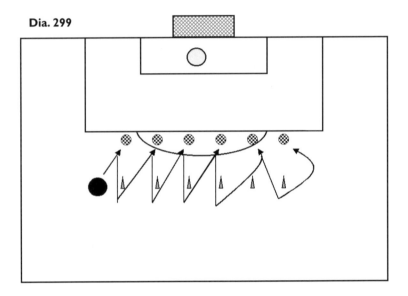

• In this exercise a player outside the area sprints towards the cone and then makes a swift turn away, freeing himself of marking before gaining possession of a ball passed to him by a teammate. The coach gives the signal that starts each movement, calling out the name of the player who is to pass the ball. When he hears his teammate's name called out, the player who is to shoot starts to run towards the cone, choosing at the last moment the direction to change to in order to receive the pass. In this exercise the coach should comment, not only on the actual shot at goal, but also on the direction the striker chooses to take when he is freeing himself and on his way of receiving the pass. (diagram 300)

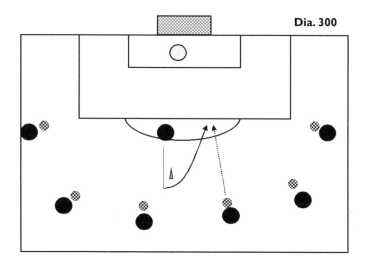

Dia. 300

• Six players and two goalkeepers face each other on a small field with normal goals. A line divides the field in two to separate the plays of the backs and the strikers. The backs must mark the strikers, and pass the ball to their own strikers without being able to cross the line that divides the field in two. When they have regained possession they cannot be approached by their opposing strikers unless they are inside the area. Neither can the strikers go over the dividing line to give a hand to their own backs in defense. The small field, the team divided in two sectors, the opportunities to create continuous attacking plays − all these things should train the strikers in freeing themselves of marking and in shooting at goal. The winning team is the one that scores more goals in a determined period of time. Goals scored by strikers who regain possession from balls pushed away by the keeper before the backs can intercept are to be considered valid. (diagram 301)

Dia. 301

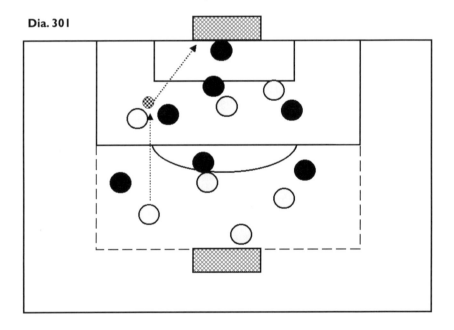

EXERCISES IN GROUP TACTICS.

We have shown from the very beginning of this book how the attacking phase can be divided into various sub phases (plays after gaining possession of the ball, build up of play, final touches and shooting); and we have looked at the finishing touch plays used to arrive at a shot on goal. Exercises in group tactics are done in order to encourage the team to improve the strengths that will allow the players to achieve the tactical aims connected with the achievement of the various sub phases. The actual exercise used during training in group tactics are what we call 'theme training matches', i.e., matches in which the basic rules of the game of soccer are changed or adapted so that the team can try to develop certain plays that the coach considers relevant. The 'theme training matches' that we wish to propose set out to improve, not only the individual's technical \ tactical ability in situations that are similar to those of a real match, but also the team's knowledge of and competence in:

- handling the post possession phase;
- organizing the build-up phase;
- managing to counter attack with speed;
- choosing between the many possible finishing touch plays.

EXERCISES FOR IMPROVING BALL MANAGEMENT AFTER REGAINING POSSESSION OF THE BALL

• Two teams face each other inside a delimited area. Each player has been given an opponent who he must mark in an aggressive way. The exercise begins with the coach who throws up the ball into a random part of the field. The team whose player has regained possession must complete three passes in order to score a point. Every time the opponents manage to regain possession, the ball will be given back to the coach to start again. (diagram 302)

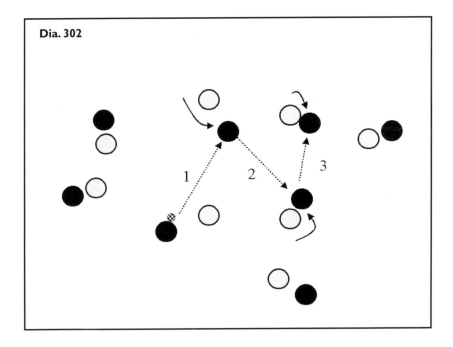

Dia. 302

• Two teams of eleven players face each other on a normal-sized field, as in the diagram, with the midfield sections drawn up around their own half way line.

The coach throws the ball into one of the two team's defending halves.

When this defending section has received the ball, its job is to begin an attacking play, trying to escape the opponents' pressing, which must be continuous and sustained.

If the team in possession manages to bring the ball over the mid-field line they get a point; when they bring the ball up to finishing touch play, they get two points; and if they actually manage to score a goal they will be awarded five points. At the end, the team that has the highest number of points will win. Clearly, when the defending team manages to regain possession, the ball will be given back to the coach to begin the exercise again. (diagram 303)

Dia. 303

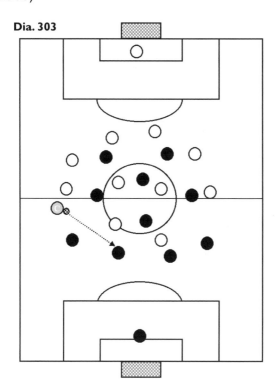

EXERCISES FOR IMPROVING BUILD-UP.

• Three teams in different colored vests face each other in a delimited area.
These three groups have to collaborate among themselves, passing each other the ball according to the following rules: the player in possession must pass the ball immediately (i.e., without being marked) to a teammate with a vest of a different color from his own and also from that of the player from whom he received it. The player must also be in movement (i.e., not standing still) as he receives the ball. This exercise for improving ball possession is important because it highlights playing tempo both with the ball and without it. It also encourages the players to move in unison. (diagram 304)

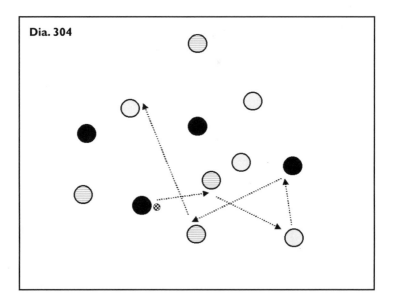

Dia. 304

• Classic exercise with regard to ball possession.: the team gains a point when they manage to carry out a certain number of passes without letting their opponents intercept. If this exercise is done with intensity – and because it is carried out without interruptions –it can also help the players in terms of physical fitness. (diagram 305)

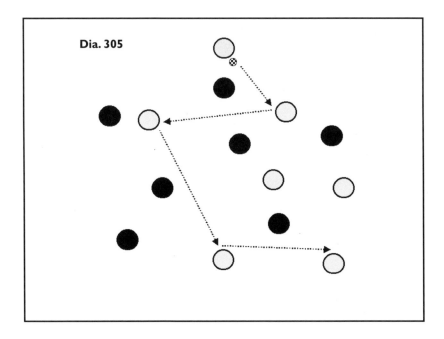

Dia. 305

• There are the same number of mini goals in the work area as there are members of each team. To gain a point, the player in possession must pass the ball through the stakes to a player on his own team (diagram 306)

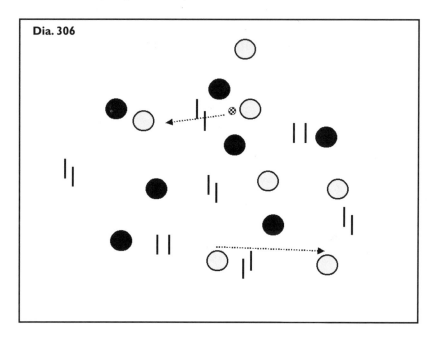

Dia. 306

• Two teams face each other in the work area playing a match that has one special rule. The team that scores a goal gains a point only if they can then make a certain number of passes without their opponents being able to intercept. They can gain this point at any time from the moment they actually score until the moment that their opponents score another goal. In a situation where the team that has scored is unable to 'confirm' this with its ensuing ball possession, but has, on the contrary, conceded a goal – then, of course, the tables will be turned on them. Now it is their opponents who will have to 'confirm' their goal, while the team that scored before have lost their point and will have to prevent their opponents from carrying out the determined number of passes and try to score another goal in order to put themselves in advantage.

• Two teams face each other in the work area, both forced to play vertically in the defense section. This exercise helps to train players in building up with long passes or with vertical passes followed by a dump. This may be important when teaching the team to look for alternative solutions during build-up or to prepare them for a match if their opponents are good at offensive pressing and you think they may be able to sink your own team too far back into their own midfield. (diagram 307)

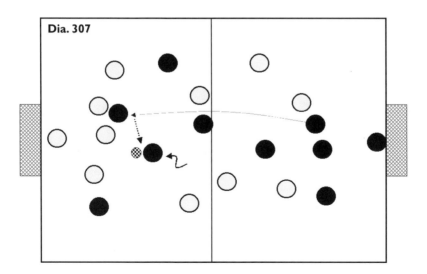

EXERCISES FOR IMPROVING RAPID COUNTER ATTACKS.

• In this exercise the two teams gain a point when, after having made a prescribed number of passes, the players manage to bring the ball beyond their opponents' defense line within a limited number of seconds.

This exercise aims to show the players how to attack with speed after they have consolidated their possession. It also gets them used to varying playing rhythm. (diagram 308)

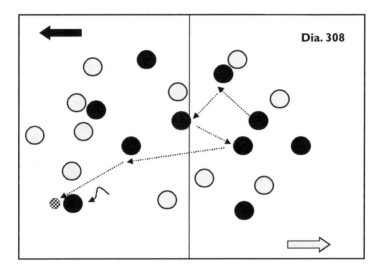

• In this exercise two teams face each other in a small field, each having a limited number of seconds to score a goal after they have gained possession.

To do this, they must alternate plays and change situations as rapidly as possible, and this will get them used to developing their playing rhythms and will also help to speed up passing from one to another.

• The coach asks the backs and midfielders from the training team (team A) to move the ball about, following the type of plays normally used by the team during build-up.

The midfielders and the strikers on team B move in relation to the motion of the ball, simulating pressing.

At the sign from the coach the player on team B nearest to the ball, will stop simulating and go to take the ball (helped by the team A player who will let him step in). At this point (i.e., when any player on team B gets possession of the ball) the real exercise will begin, with the attacking players striking as quickly as they can, exploiting the fact that the players on team A are all spread out because they have previously been trying to build up attacking play. This exercise aims to encourage attacking players to counter attack with speed, but it also shows the players of team B that they must streamline their positions at once when they have lost possession so that they can defend their opponents.

(see diagrams 309 and 310 on next page)

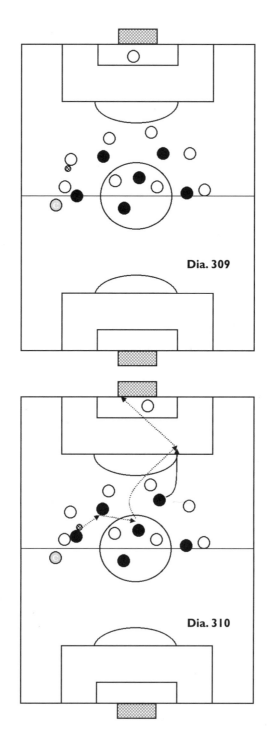

Dia. 309

Dia. 310

EXERCISES FOR IMPROVING FINISHING TOUCH TECHNIQUES.

To help your team learn how to use the complete range of finishing touch plays in relation to the tactical situation on the field it is a good idea to make them play 'theme training matches' in which two teams (made up of a minimum of seven players each, lined up in three divisions) face each other with the aim of scoring goals. In this case, however, goal scoring must take place as the result of predetermined types of finishing touch plays, which should be different for each team in order that the players can combine and get an overall view of various tactical situations.

• **Theme training match for improving finishing touch techniques like overlapping and in-depth cuts.**
Team W (white) can shoot after an in-depth cross created by overlapping.
Team B (black) can score a goal only after an assist created by an in-depth cut.
To make this a little easier we can set up the following rules:

    1) The marked zone can be defended only by a team B side back. This rule helps to give numerical superiority on the sides and encourages team W players to look for crosses coming from overlapping on the sidelines.

    2) For a team W goal to be valid, the whole team (except the goalkeeper, of course) must be in the attacking half of the field when it is scored. This will encourage team B's counter attacks, giving them space from which to proceed.

    3) Team B will be able to press and steal balls only in their own half. This rule favors team W's forward movement and gives team B players the chance to attack space in depth.

    4) When they have gained possession, team B players have only a limited number of seconds before they must shoot at goal. This rule forces team B players to counter attack quickly using long passes into open space directed at the strikers. (diagram 311)

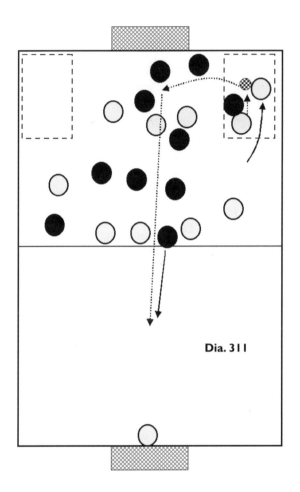

Dia. 311

• Theme training match for improving finishing touch techniques like dump and rebound passes or attacking free space.

Team B aims to shoot at goal after a dump and rebound from a striker.

Team W can shoot only after a player with the ball at his feet has attacked whatever space he finds.

> 1) Beyond the horizontal line marked on the field team B can only use one-touch play. This is to encourage dump and rebound passes.
>
> 2) When team W midfielders have received the ball beyond the other horizontal line they must try repeatedly to penetrate their opponent's defense in a vertical line for at least ten yards. This will encourage them to break into the attacking zone with the ball at their feet. (diagram 312)

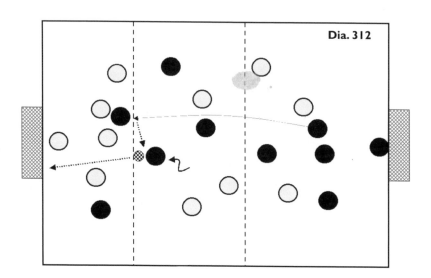

Dia. 312

• Theme training match for improving finishing touch techniques like combinations and dribbling.
Team B can only score a goal from combinations (give and go, give and follow or dummies) between teammates.
Team W's goals must be the result of the player in possession dribbling past his direct opponent and shooting or passing to a teammate who is in a better position than him.

1) Players on team B can only shoot when they are inside the marked line. Inside that line they can also carry out one-touch plays.
2) It is not possible to double up on team W players inside the marked rectangles, where team W players can, if they consider it possible, try to dribble past their direct opponents. (diagram 313)

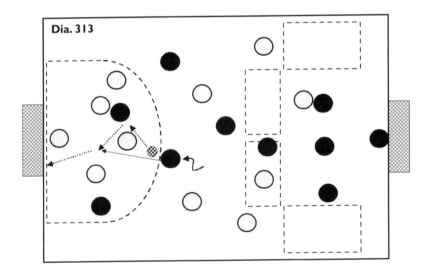

Dia. 313

• **Theme training match for improving finishing touch techniques like crossing from depth or, alternatively, shooting from outside the area.**

Both teams have the same aim in this exercise: shooting at goal after a cross from the end line or, as an alternative, from outside the area.

Four rectangles are marked on the field (diag. 314). Players must cross from these in the attempt to set up a shot on goal.

The following rule will help the attacking team to develop finishing touch play from crosses:

> 1) The side midfielders on each team can only play an attacking game, i.e., they will defend in a passive way.

This will create numerical superiority on the sides for the team in possession. The fact that the teams can also score by shooting from outside the area will vary the plays carried out by the attacking team as well as stopping the center midfielders from going to the sides to defend. Goals can also be scored from outside the area as a result of stealing a ball cleared by the backs after a cross. (diagram 314)

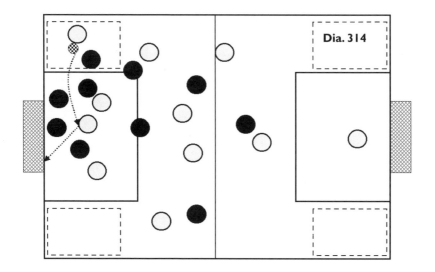

Dia. 314

• Theme training match for improving ability to attack a traditional or a zonal defense system.
Two teams face each other on the field, one marking men and the other using zonal defense. Both teams try to set up the best finishing touch plays to break open the opponents' defense. The team attacking a defense that is marking man-to-man will have to:

1) put the striker near the sweeper (diag. 315) so that the defense player finds it more difficult to cover play;

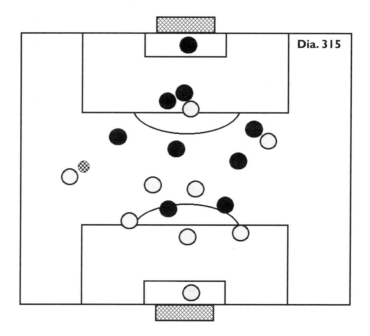

Dia. 315

2) make the strikers move about a lot so that the backs marking them are forced to follow them around, thus freeing space to be broken into by the midfielders. (diagram 316)

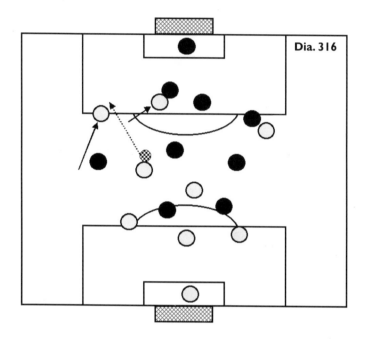

Dia. 316

At the same time, the team playing against a zonal defense will try to attack by:

1) diagonal cuts between side and center players, i.e., on the blind side of the center back; (diagram 317)

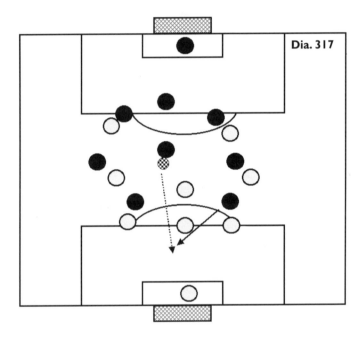

Dia. 317

2) cuts made to spread out the strikers on the opposite side to where the ball is; (diagram 318)

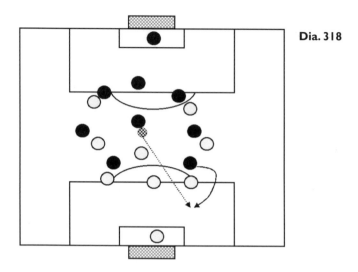

Dia. 318

3) the midfielders moving up to spaces occupied by the strikers in order to create numerical superiority. (diagram 319)

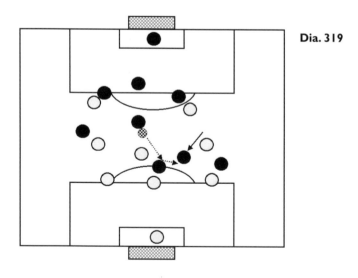

Dia. 319

LEARNING THE SYSTEM.

If a team wants to play organized and exciting soccer, each player must understand to perfection the tactical system chosen by his coach, and his single duties within that system, both when his team is in possession and when it is not. After having established his team's guiding philosophy and overall strategy, the coach must also organize his team's general attacking phase by making sure that the player in possession always has the greatest number of choices open to him from which he can select the most suitable. If the player in possession is to be able to choose between the greatest number of opportunities possible, his teammates without the ball must always be on the move with the right tempo and following the types of attacking plays that the coach has foreseen for them. The following exercises aim to help the players understand the different types of plays and the mechanics of their particular playing system, and then to expand these indications into active play against real opponents in competitive situations.

EXERCISES FOR SPECIFIC SECTIONS IN ORDER TO PERFECT THE PLAYERS UNDERSTANDING OF THE VARIOUS POSSIBLE SOLUTIONS IN BUILD-UP AND FINISHING TOUCH SITUATIONS.

• The defense and midfield sections of the team are lined up in the defending half of the field according to the pre-established system without any opponent in front of them.
The coach gives the ball to the goalkeeper or to any other player, who, in collaboration with his teammates, must bring it beyond the midfield line using the build-up plays that the coach has already indicated.
The coach must observe the overall flow of play and he must make sure that the passes are precise from the point of view of speed and direction; that teammates are supporting the player in possession, giving him at all times the easy chance to dump the ball; and that the players who receive do so in movement, in a way that simulates the act of freeing themselves of marking.
When the players have gained confidence with the playing

schemes and when they have learned the movements by heart, some opponents will be put on to face them on the field, and this will make the exercise more and more complex and complete.

• The midfield and the attacking sections are lined up in the attacking half according to the pre-established system without any opponents in front of them.
The two (or three, depending on the system) center midfielders are passing the ball to each other waiting for the signal from the coach.
When he gives the signal, the midfielder in possession will tell his teammates to begin the attack.
At first, it will be a good idea if the players arrive to the point where they can shoot following the coach's indications.
When the players and the team as a whole have learned the movements and the plays by heart, then they should be left free to interpret the situation, choosing the finishing touch play that seems best to them at the moment.
As the team goes on improving, the exercise can be made more difficult but putting some opponents onto the field.
First of all, backs can be sent in to mark the players, then mid-fielders and backs in cover.

TEAM EXERCISES

11 AGAINST THE GOALKEEPER.
The whole team is lined up on the entire playing field. The players must carry out attacking plays without any opposition, except the goalkeeper defending the goal under fire. At the end of each play, the players return to their original positions, ready to begin another attacking maneuver. This is an important exercise with a view to giving players a complete vision of how attacking plays must work. The team has to develop play going from build-up to finishing touches and then shooting. The coach must consider the overall flow of play, paying careful attention to the precision of the passes and the tempo of the movements of the players in support.

You can begin the exercise in different ways:
• The coach gives the ball to the goalkeeper of the team that he is training and so play will begin from the back. (diagram 320)

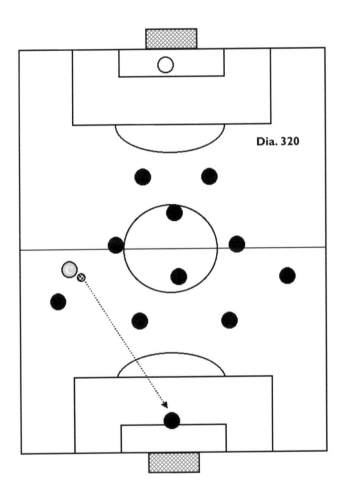

Dia. 320

• The ball is put in play by a clearing kick from the opposing goal-keeper. (diagram 321)

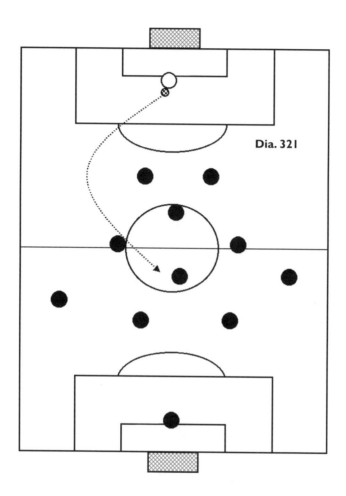

Dia. 321

• The coach passes the ball to any player, whose job it will then be to start attacking play. (diagram 322)

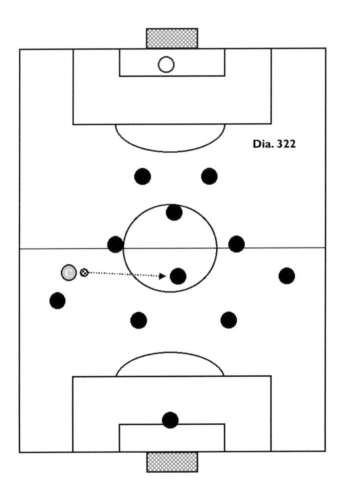

Dia. 322

• The coach asks the team to simulate the defense phase, indicating the movements to be made (doubling up, moving back, etc.). At this point he throws the ball on the field, telling the player nearest to it to take possession and start a rapid counter attack.

In the first of these situations (dia. 323), attacking play will require elaborate build-up; in the last (dia. 324) we are trying to improve the team's ability to get into a position to shoot as quickly as they can – and here it is not necessary that play begins from behind.

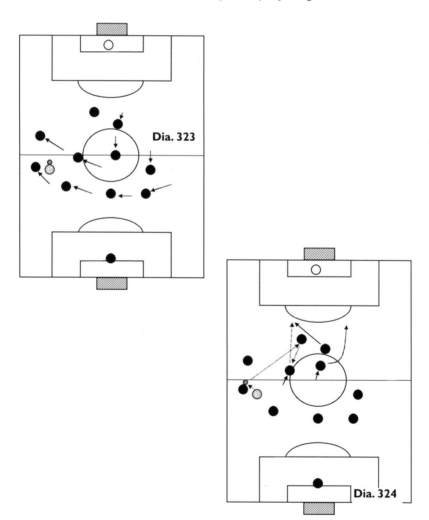

Dia. 323

Dia. 324

The coach can also vary the administration of the exercise in order to keep the training session fresh and stimulating, which, in turn, will make it easier to improve what still needs correcting, and polish up the techniques that have already been learned.

• As they are learning how to carry out the plays, the coach will give the players precise details about how to move, which he will explain to them before the training session actually begins.
• When the team has shown that they have grasped the plays and can use them in good symmetry, the coach can then expect the players to arrive to the point where they can shoot at goal using one or other of the finishing touch techniques that he has illustrated to them without him having to tell them exactly which.

The coach could also add some other rules:

• The team has to finish the play within a precise number of seconds.
• They can only pass the ball a certain number of times before they shoot.
• Distribute different colored vests to the 11 players, telling them, for example, that play must develop alternating the color of the player in possession. (diagram 325)
• The coach could intervene directly in the exercise with a whistle. This sign could mean that the player in possession cannot bring play forward, but that he has to dump the ball on a supporting player. It could also have the opposite meaning: that the player has open space in front of him and can go up and enter into the finishing touch phase.
• Place some obstacles on the field which would make the transmission phase a little more complex, and would force the players without the ball to make runs and turns to free themselves of marking.
• Put 10 opponents on the field, apart from the goalkeeper (and in the places of the obstacles). These would have to act in a passive way, having been told that they are not to intervene on the ball unless it arrives in the position they have been given.

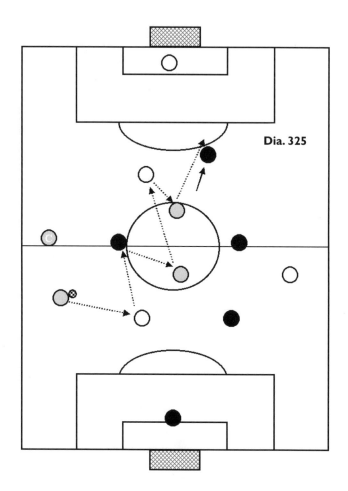

Dia. 325

11 AGAINST THE OPPONENTS' DEFENSE SECTION (THREE OR FOUR BACKS AND THE GOALKEEPER).

This exercise is similar to the last, with the difference that, in order to get to a point where they can shoot, the team will have to avoid the intervention of the opposing backs, who will now be playing in an active way. This exercise allows the team to play without problems during build-up, while, of course, during the finishing touch phase, and, in particular, when they are trying to shoot, the rhythm, the direction of the assist and the way in which the striker frees himself from marking – all these things will now have to be perfect. (diagram 326)

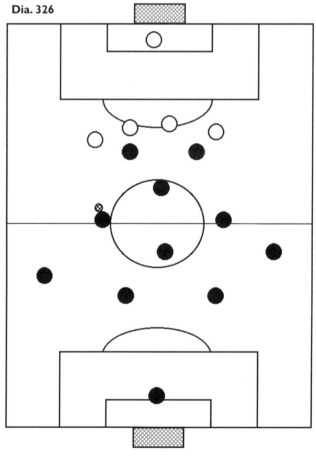

Dia. 326

11 AGAINST THE DEFENSE AND THE MIDFIELD SECTIONS (SEVEN OR EIGHT PLAYERS AND THE GOALKEEPER).

This time the players will have to elude the resistance of their opponents' midfielders and backs. Of course the backs will still be able to build up in limited freedom, but finishing touches and shooting at goal will be carried out in conditions exactly like those of a real match. The exercise can follow the same rules as the last (i.e., whenever the attacking play of the 11 arrives to a conclusion, they begin again by returning to their original positions with one of their players in possession or by giving goals to the team in numerical inferiority (for example, that they must bring the ball over a particular line on the field) so as to create an exercise without interruptions. (diagram 327)

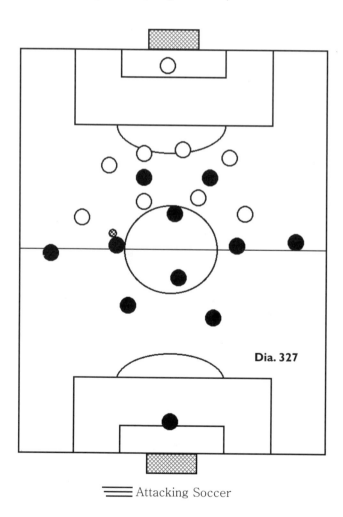

Dia. 327

11 AGAINST 11.

The concluding exercise is the classical, but fundamental, training match (or friendly match) 11 against 11.
Like the others, this match can be carried out following special rules in order to get the team to play with certain distinct aims in mind.
The other team could be a sort of sparring partner, using a system similar to the one adopted by the team they are to meet in the next official match. We could also ask our players to:
• Build up or arrive to the finishing touch phase using, for the most part, certain pre-arranged techniques.
• Shoot at goal within a limited number of seconds.
• Shoot at goal within a limited number of passes.
(diagram 328)

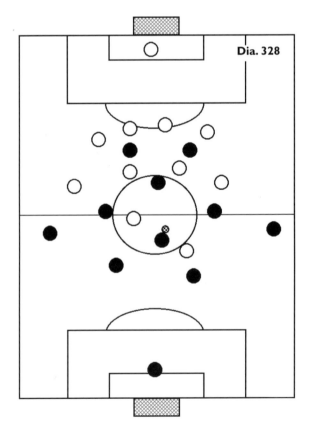

Dia. 328

8

AN <u>OVERALL</u> <u>SURVEY</u> <u>AND</u> <u>SOME</u> POSSIBLE TACTICAL <u>MODIFICATIONS</u> <u>WITH</u> <u>A</u> <u>VIEW</u> <u>TO</u> IMPROVING <u>THE</u> <u>ATTACKING</u> PHASE

AN OVERALL SURVEY OF THE ATTACKING PHASE.

Having now listed the most important tactical aspects of the attacking phase and having had a detailed look at some attacking plays in reference to the different systems in use, we can now concentrate our attention on the tactical changes that the coach can make during the match in order to refine the attacking power of his team.

In order to analyze our team's effectiveness, we must repeat an important concept: ball possession is not an independent thing, but is closely connected with non-possession – so that the way we attack will condition the way we defend and vice versa.

The all important points which a coach will have to consider when he makes a survey of his team's attacking play are these:

1. the influence of the defense play on the attacking phase
2. the quality of the attacking phase:
     – an analysis of build-up
     – an analysis of finishing touch play
     – an analysis of how plays are concluded

In reference to point number one, it is obvious that the phase of non-possession conditions the way in which our team will counter attack. If our team is feeling the pressure too much in defense, then the players will probably regain possession somewhere near their goal or in the penalty area, and that in turn will probably bring about a drop off in playing standards (especially if our players are not good with the ball). A completely different situation is when our players are good at dribbling and at keeping possession, (or better, at least, than their opposite numbers). In cases like this, there is no point in going in for ultra-offensive pressing because that would only take depth out of the counter attack.

These two examples are enough to outline the importance and the influence of a good defense strategy on the force and quality of attacking play.

In relation to point number two, the coach must define what he considers the best attacking plays, tactically speaking, to put his opponents under pressure – and to do so he will of course have to assess the particular strengths of his team.

Generally speaking, this will mean deciding whether to use elaborate maneuvers or quick break away plays, diagonal or long passes and whether to get into a position for shooting by using crosses, cuts, dump and rebound passes, dribbling, shots from far out or combinations.

Now let's have a closer look at what it means to make an overall survey of the build-up phase.

Both as he prepares for the match and as it is being played, the coach must decide the best way of building up play.

His decisions on how the team is to build up play depends on the technical strength of the players and the placement of the two teams on the field of play. In order to build up attacking play with confidence, the defense section must be made up of players who are technically competent and who can play in numerical superiority to the strikers who will try to prevent them moving the ball around at the back.

When either or both of these two factors are not in evidence, it might be a good idea to change our type of build-up play and choose another that we do not normally apply.

On the other hand, when we build up play by using long passes, we need players good at kicking into depth, of course, but their front line teammates will also need more elevation than their direct opponents. In cases where these two factors are clearly not in our team's favor we should consider modifying the way in which we intend to build up play.

Apart from this, the coach can also change the situation on the field either by substituting one or more players or by altering the system of play.

An exchange of players or a substitution, or the variation of the entire system of play can improve the technical strength of the section of the team in question, giving the players the chance to get over the problems they have been meeting up to then.

Turning to the survey of the finishing touch phase, we must be sure that the team is exploiting all its strengths and is also hitting the opponents where they are at their weakest. The coach must make sure, on the one hand, that the players are utilizing the finishing touch plays that come most naturally to them, and, on the other, that they are attacking in the most productive fashion. The coach's most important duty will be to suggest the most effective ways of breaking up their opponent's defense system, but he will also have to substitute players or modify the tactical set up when the team is not playing at its best.

It is important to ask ourselves if the way in which we serve the strikers is really effective or not, and also, just how dangerous are the attempts the strikers are making to shoot at goal. For example, if the striker does not have as much elevation as the back covering him, it does no good for him to take up position inside the area waiting for a cross. Similarly, if the attacking player keeps failing to dribble past his opponent, there is no point in him insisting, and he should make himself more useful with dump and rebound passes or diagonal cuts that will create space for his teammates. In conclusion, in order to judge the offensive power of the team, we must try to understand if it is attacking in the best possible way in relation to the strikers' ability to put the opponents' individual players or their whole defensive system under constant pressure.

For an in-depth assessment of finishing touch play, the coach must also consider the team's overall ability in bringing forward and supporting play without leaving the opponents freedom to counter attack as they wish. If, for example, the opponents' attacking players have good elevation and they keep receiving crosses from the sidelines, we must ask the side midfielders to move up into attack as often as they can so that the players who are covering them will be forced to move back and will not be able to break into spaces from which they can cross into the area. On the other hand, if our opponents are attacking with a couple of players using spaces opening up to them in counter attack, we must tell our midfielders to get between them and not allow them too much freedom of maneuver in such situations.

CHANGES MADE TO IMPROVE THE TEAM'S PERFORMANCE.

When the coach has a clear idea about what is happening on the field, he must then make the counter moves so that his team can confront and break open their opponent's strategy.

The best possible playing conditions for a soccer team is when they are in a situation of clear superiority in defense and in attack. When, in other words, the team can interrupt their opponents' attacking play, easily regaining possession, and at the same time are making constantly dangerous attacking moves. In situations like these, the coach will merely keep his eye out that his team is continuing to dominate, intervening only in cases of dire necessity (injury, for example).
Most often, however, the match will be in the balance, and the coach's interventions will be made in order to improve either the defense or the attacking play. We have already seen that an improvement (or, for that matter, a deterioration) of our team's attacking power will greatly influence the defense phase or vice versa. The changes that the coach makes must improve one of the two phases, naturally; but it is equally important that it does not do so by creating problems in the opposite section of the team. It is much easier to explain what is meant with an example: if an extra striker is put on in order to make the team's attacking play more effective, it is important that they should maintain their performance in defense; and, on the other hand, if the coach inserts a back to improve the performance in defense, the team must still be able to counter attack when the opportunity presents itself.

If we come now to looking at the possible moves that a coach can make, we will see at once that he can improve the performance of his team by making the following changes:

• inverting the position of two (or more) players on the field
• putting on a substitute
• varying the team's pre-defined strategy by bring up or lowering the line where the team begins pressing.
• modifying the system by changing the position (moving forward

or backward) of one or more players, or inserting a new player in the place of another

All these moves are ways of improving our team's ability to confront the opponent, and can have an important effect on the team's center of balance.

We can now have a look at some standard situations, and the tactical moves that the coach can make in order to improve the situation.

SITUATION: our team is sunk back into its own half. This allows the opponents to build up dangerous play with continuity while at the same time inhibiting our ability to counter attack.

BASIC SOLUTION: bring up the center of balance.

POSSIBLE MOVES:

1) The first thing the coach must do is to regulate the way in which the team is marking. Players who are in difficulty can change places or be substituted so as to limit the most dangerous players on the opposing team.
2) The system can be modified by bringing an attacking player further back, or by putting on a midfielder or a back in the place of a striker in order to improve the overall quality of the defense and gain space on the field of play.
3) If none of the above moves has the desired effect, or, in any case, in order to integrate his team's productivity, the coach can substitute the striker on the field with another who is better able to exploit whatever spaces there may be.

We could also try to rectify the situation by improving our team's performance in attack. If he wants to run a risk, the coach could even insert an extra striker, telling his team, thrown back around their area, to use long passes, allowing the strikers to go into depth or the center midfielder to give dump and rebound passes to the teammates of his section so that they can move the whole team forward. The insertion of an extra striker may also damage the opponent's tactical line up, diminishing the fluidity of their play and taking the pressure off our defense. Another thing that might be useful is to put a midfielder on, particularly one who is good at keeping possession: and this is another way of bringing the team out and up.

SITUATION: it is a balanced match but we just cannot manage to be concretely dangerous.

BASIC SOLUTION: improve our attacking play.

POSSIBLE MOVES:

1) Ask our team to use finishing touch techniques that they have not tried up to now.
2) Change the position of the strikers.
3) Make substitutions role by role. We can put on a striker in the place of a teammate from the same section, or we can insert a midfielder with attacking inclinations suitable to the type of match that we are playing, in substitution of a teammate from the same section.

We can ask our team to bring the center of balance up or down by redefining the line where they begin pressing. In this way we give ourselves greater or lesser space and we are making the best of our strikers' attacking characteristics. The drawback of a move like this is that it can favor our opponents' play as well.

SITUATION: we are in control of play but we just can't clinch the result.

BASIC SOLUTION: increase the attacking sector's effectiveness.

POSSIBLE MOVES:

1) Alternate the strikers' position.
2) Insert a striker with different characteristics from the one playing at the beginning of the match.
3) Put on an extra striker.
4) Change finishing touch play. It may even be a good idea to allow our opponents to come forward so that we can exploit the space opening up behind them.

SITUATION: our team is on top, but our opponents are back in the match and we are suffering.

BASIC SOLUTION: we must give confidence to the defense section; and, at the same time, the team must be able to counter attack in a forceful way.

POSSIBLE MOVES:

1) If the match is nearly over, it might be a good idea to strengthen the defense or the midfield by taking off a striker and thus modifying the system.
2) On the other hand, if there is still a long time to go, we must, first of all, try to foresee if our opponents' superiority is likely to last or if it is the result of a momentary effort. In the second case, we could try to resist without changing the line up of the team, maybe asking the strikers to participate more in the defense phase. However, if the opponents' prevalence looks likely to continue, we must try to bring up the team's center of balance by modifying the system. Putting on another striker or a mid-

fielder who likes to go into attack might be a risk, but it is often a valid solution. There is no point, I think, putting on an extra back when a large part of the match still has to be played. A move like that would block any chance of winning the match should our opponents manage to score a drawing goal.

SITUATION: our team is a goal down, and continues to feel the pressure.

BASIC SOLUTION: keep the match on the boil.

POSSIBLE MOVES:

When we are facing players who are stronger or in better form than us, the most important thing is to keep the match alive – so that we will have every chance of getting a positive result. What we must try to do, in fact, is to make our bid in the last quarter hour of the game, when the risk of taking a second goal is compensated by the possibility that our own team might just score a goal and draw the match.

1) If there is still a long time to go and our team is under pressure, it is not a mistake to put on a defender, so as to contain the disadvantage of a single goal. Of course that kind of attitude will have to change radically in the last part of the match when the team will be doing everything they can to get a drawing goal.
2) If the match is nearing its conclusion we must insert an extra striker to force the tactical situation.

CONCLUSION

This book is not a manual of attacking play; it proposes, rather, to be a means to the end of encouraging everyone to study and enrich their knowledge of this exciting aspect of the game. As in daily life, so in sport: building is always much more complicated than destroying. So it is that we can have full and unqualified admiration and respect for teams that play constructive soccer – and this will very often go well beyond the mere result of a single match.

One last point remains to be made: the brilliance and the force of a team's attacking phase depends entirely on the quality of the players the coach can choose from. Apart from being able to judge and evaluate the principle players that make up his team, and as well as trying to 'construct' plays that will put those individuals in a position to express themselves at their very best, the intelligent coach will also dedicate much of his time and energy to the improvement of his players' technical and tactical strengths during training sessions.